Commitment and Responsibility in Nursing

A Faith-Based Approach

IN ASSOCIATION WITH

Prof. Dr. G.A. Lindeboom Institute
Ede, The Netherlands
        www.lindeboominstituut.nl

Center for Bioethics and Public Policy
London, United Kingdom
        www.cbpp.ac.uk

Center for Bioethics and Human Dignity
Bannockburn, IL, United States
        www.cbhd.org

and

Nurses Christian Fellowship International
        http://welcome.to/ncfi

Commitment and Responsibility in Nursing

A Faith-Based Approach

Edited by

Bart Cusveller, Agneta Sutton, Dónal O'Mathúna

Dordt College Press, Sioux Center, Iowa

Printed in the United States of America.

Dordt College Press   www.dordt.edu/dordt_press
498 Fourth Avenue NE
Sioux Center, Iowa 51250
United States of America
ISBN: 0-932914-51-9

Library of Congress Cataloging-in-Publication Data

Commitment and responsibility in nursing : a faith-based approach /
edited by Bart Cusveller, Agneta Sutton, Dónal O'Mathúna.
    p. ; cm.
Includes bibliographical references.
  ISBN 0-932914-51-9 (pbk. : alk. paper)
 1. Nursing ethics. 2. Christian ethics. 3. Nursing ethics--Religious
aspects--Christianity.
  [DNLM: 1. Ethics, Nursing. 2. Christianity. 3. Professional Role.
4. Religion and Medicine. WY 85 C7338 2003] I. Cusveller, B. S. (Bart
S.) II. Sutton, Agneta. III. O'Mathúna, Dónal.
  RT85.C65 2004
  174.2--dc22   2003025627

Cover design by Jessica Van Smeerdyk
Copy editing by Kim Rylaarsdam

Contents

Preface

Are Christian nurses any different from other nurses?

Do nurses who profess to be Christians have different responsibilities from other nurses?

Well, Christians do see the world, themselves, and their fellow beings in a special light. Christians see the world in the light of God: the creator, the redeemer, and the one who sustains, loves, and holds the world and everything and everybody. Christians see the world, themselves, and their fellow beings in the light of temporality, i.e., Christians are "on the way."

This perspective gives Christian nurses a different responsibility and calls for a different commitment. What this responsibility entails and how such a commitment is expressed in concrete nursing action is unfolded in this book.

Agneta Sutton, Bart Cusveller, and Dónal O'Mathúna have edited a textbook on nursing ethics with a difference. Together with six internationally well-known authors, they confront us about this different and special Christian perspective.

As we adjust to living in the third millennium, questions of societal values are more frequently asked and debated. In this context discussions over health care ethics occupy an increasing prominence, demonstrated by the number of new publications in this area. But these public debates on values rarely result in clear answers.

This book presents an open and unabashed delineation of Christian values as they apply to nurses and nursing. When possible, readers will find clear answers and positions. The authors, however, do not hesitate to admit that Christians do not always possess solutions to conflicts and dilemmas.

The three parts of the book focus on different aspects. The first part centers on the Christian origins of nursing and on the faith from which traditional nursing values originated. The following part discusses specific relationships involving nurses and patients, nurse colleagues, and other health care professionals. This part builds on the foundations laid in the foregoing chapters. The last three chapters focus on particular problems raised in situations involving terminal care, patients' sexuality, and alternative therapies.

The authors state, "The core of nursing is rooted in the Christian tradition" (2). To bear witness to this tradition in their work, Christian nurses will engage and try to make a difference. This calling is not easy. The authors share their experience and ability for reflection as they relate professional action to our religious background. The authors "are seeking to provide the tools and attitudes that Christian nurses need to engage in debate and dialogue with the world around them" (10).

Such tools are provided in this book! It does not outline a straightforward and simplistic Christian perspective on health care ethics. Instead, it relates concrete nursing situations to the general demands of the nursing profession and asks for a specific nursing response from a professional with a Christian perspective. Any reader will benefit from the open and intrepid discussions. We can easily see that for a committed Christian, good and ethical nursing practice intrinsically embraces general professionalism. And this point is an important message to nurses who want to live their faith as professionals: the respect for human dignity lies at the roots of any nursing action. The difference is found in the belief that as Christians we know that "human dignity derives from the fact that each one of us—whatever our shortcomings and weaknesses—is created in the image of God" (3).

Sr. Marianne Benedicta (Prof. Dr. Arndt)
University for Applied Sciences
Neubrandenburg, Germany

1

Introduction

Commitment and responsibility in nursing

Agneta Sutton and Bart Cusveller

1. The basic question

What does it mean to be a Christian in today's world of nursing? This is the fundamental question addressed by the contributors to this volume. Their focus is on nursing ethics. While there are numerous books on nursing ethics today, few of them seek to formulate a specifically Christian understanding of the nursing profession. Our aim is to help Christian nurses towards a self-understanding that will promote confidence in their Christian values and assist them in articulating and defending those values in their often secular working environments.

As Christians, nurses see the world as created, fallen, and redeemed through the Lord Jesus. They see life as a pilgrimage towards the Kingdom of God, an understanding of the world revealed in the Holy Scriptures. Even if individual Christians and Christian denominations differ in some beliefs, all Christians share a belief in a loving God, who sent his Son to die for us sinners, and who is calling us to bear witness to this Gospel news. Jesus Christ, whom we meet in the Gospels and read about in the letters of St. Paul and the other New Testament writers, is the focal point of our belief as Christians. He asks all of us to follow Him and bear witness to His good news about the Kingdom to come. All Christians, then, share in the understanding that human worth and dignity derives from the fact that each one of us–however incapacitated and sinful–is created in the image of God. We were all created to be in intimate relationship with one another and with God Himself. We are all called by the greatest commandment to love God and our neighbors. It follows from these beliefs that human life is not ours to take but to be cared for and cherished in each and every one of us until it comes to a natural end. Nursing is thus ultimately one way of loving our fellow human neighbors.

But how can nurses reconcile their responsibility as Christians with that of modern professional nurses? The nursing profession has changed over time, especially in the last few decades. Nurses have become more aware of their professional status. They have become more assertive vis-à-vis the medical profession. They have made scholarly attempts to carve out a special image for themselves as professionals with special skills and responsibilities. In many countries, nurses are training at higher levels than before and taking on duties such as prescribing medication as well as performing surgical procedures and giving general anesthetics, duties that were formerly the prerogative of the medical profession. In addition, nursing is no longer an exclusively female profession and medicine is no longer as male dominated as it was. There is more emphasis on teamwork today than in the past when the nurse tended to be treated as little more than a handmaid of the doctor.

Even with these changes, the core of nursing is rooted in the Christian tradition. It is rooted in Christian values. And as a practice developed in the Christian tradition, the central task of nursing is caring. Indeed, the very word "nursing" points to this. To nurse is to care for the weak and vulnerable and helpless. The word "hospital" points in the same direction. This word is derived from the Latin for *welcome*. The hospitals of old welcomed the weak, the sick, and the needy. Those who worked in the hospitals (mostly members of female religious communities) cared for those who sought help and shelter. Theirs was a vocation. They felt called to serve God by serving their neighbors. As a practice and profession of Christian origin, nursing remains a vocation in the sense of a practice requiring and fostering devotion to the sick, weak, and helpless, even to the extent of performing the most humbling tasks.

What characterizes a Christian approach to nursing is the awareness of nurses being called by God to bear witness to His love for each one of us. Whatever Christian nurses do for the least of their sick sisters and brothers, they do in the name of Jesus Christ. To say this is not to say that nonchristian nurses may lack devotion and fail to recognize their work as a response to a call for help from the sick and needy. It is not to say that they cannot recognize the sick and the needy as their neighbors or that they will not respond to them with loving devotion and charity. By and large Christians and nonchristians alike will be able to work side by side for the benefit of the patient. However, nonchristian nurses will not have the same image of themselves as servants of God and neighbor, bearing witness to the redeeming love of God and the Gospel news of the Kingdom to come–and already on the way. And this worldview may mean different approaches to nursing ethics.

While the emphasis within nursing has traditionally been on the concepts of care and service, it is wrong to assume that caring excludes healing. Healing in the holistic sense means more than the promotion of physical health. However, a distinction is usually made between the medical and nursing professions in terms of healing and caring. Thus the medical profession is described as a healing profession, whereas the nursing profession is described as a caring one. But this is too sharp a distinction between the two professions. Not only do many modern nurses undertake work involving sophisticated technology and modern drugs in the service of healing, but their very nursing care must in many cases aim at and be understood as a mode of healing. For, unless the patient is incurably ill, the aim of caring is to promote greater mental and physical independence and strength, which is an aspect of healing. Conversely, to view doctors as solely healers, as opposed to carers, is to demote them to the status of technician, which depersonalizes both doctor and patient. Doctors are not mere technicians. They too have a caring role to play. Nevertheless, as a generalization, the focus of the physician is on the debilitating condition from which the patient suffers and on how to cure it or alleviate its symptoms. The nurse, on the other hand, will more often concentrate on helping the patient to function maximally in a given situation. That is to say, in an important sense nursing care involves a more personal and holistic approach. Nurses cannot but place the person, rather than his illness, in the center and by doing so they treat the patient as their neighbor. In this way Christian nurses respond to the Gospel call for charity.

As is shown in this volume, what Christian nurses, in particular, can bring to their profession and the environment in which they work is a particular understanding of the patient as a person. Given their understanding of human dignity, each and every patient must be respected and lovingly cared for, however undignified the patient's circumstances. Human dignity is not a characteristic that any of us ever loses or that some of us never possessed. Human dignity derives from the fact that each one of us–whatever our shortcomings and weaknesses–is created in the image of God. Christian

3

nurses, then, will bear witness to the dignity of the senile in their child-like helplessness. They will bear witness to the dignity of the mentally disturbed or disabled who have their own needs and desires. They will also uphold the dignity of the handicapped infant or unborn child or debilitated adult in whom others may find it difficult to recognize the personhood inherent to all human beings.

2. Outline

The volume is divided into three parts. The first part centers on the Christian origins of nursing and on the faith from which traditional nursing values originated. This part comprises the chapters written by Bart Cusveller, Ann Bradshaw, and Arlene Miller. The following part, with chapters by Kees Kleingeld, Fu-Jin Shih, and Jan van der Wolf, discusses specific relationships involving nurses and patients, nurse colleagues, and other health care professionals. This part builds on the foundations laid in the foregoing chapters. The last three chapters, by Ada van de Scheur, Bart Cusveller, and Dónal O'Mathúna, focus on particular problems raised in specific situations involving terminal care, patients' sexuality, and alternative therapies.

Each chapter is structured with a view to answering the following three questions from a Christian perspective:

- What is the nurse's professional responsibility with respect to the relationships and situations under discussion?
- What kind of ethical issues might nurses encounter in seeking to fulfill these responsibilities?
- How is the nurse to deal with these issues?

While the different contributors used a similar format, each varied in his or her approach to the topic and the focus each discussion took. Account was taken of foregoing contributions, leading to further variety. As editors, we sought to retain some evidence that this volume was designed and written by an international group; some chapters reflect this fact more than others. Furthermore, not every contributor cites biblical references to underscore his or her Christian perspective on nursing, with some contributors taking for granted well-established Christian views on responsibility, as explained in Chapter II. While some may find the examples and applications geared toward staff nurses in acute care settings, our purpose is to make contributions that are generally relevant for nurses in all practice settings. Our aim is not to produce an abstract theory or defend Christian beliefs, but to clarify the ethical responsibilities inherent to nursing as a profession and establish how Christian nurses may use those in resolving ethical problems. In other words, this book is primarily about the daily tensions the Christian nurse may encounter in practicing her profession, and how her

4

Christian faith can inform her responses so that patient well-being is promoted as much as possible. While theological arguments are not always explicit, the approach will at least be faithful to the Christian gospel.

2.1 Christian perspective on nursing ethics

The chapter by Bart Cusveller that follows this introduction is the cornerstone of the book. It advances the view that Christian nurses should bear witness to the inviolability of the human person and respect the integrity and dignity of the person whatever his or her circumstances. Entitled "What is Professional Responsibility in Nursing Practice?" it provides a Christian understanding of professional responsibility in nursing care. The author first argues that to be responsible for a certain task involves the recognition of some authority, and secondly claims that for Christians the ultimate authority is God Himself. Christian nurses, then, answer to God. Theirs is a "responsibility to make visible something of the destination of human flourishing that lies ahead of us in His coming Kingdom." As professionals, Christian nurses are, however, members of a community comprising not only Christians. This community is characterized by being a professing community. Its members profess to care for the needy and they "monitor each other's motivation, willingness, or commitment to accept the responsibility to care for those who need it." Their professional responsibility is a moral one before one another. As members of a professing community, nurses, be they Christian or not, are under a professional obligation to provide optimal care for every one of their patients. And as Christians, nurses see this requirement not only as deriving from their professional community but also as reflecting the will of God.

Nurses may also be aware that, from a historical point of view, the concept of this responsibility is of Christian origin. But not all nurses would be aware of this background. As Ann Bradshaw shows in her chapter "Changing Perceptions of Nurses' Professional Responsibility, and Lessons from the Past: A view from the United Kingdom," modern nursing has forgotten its Christian origins. The result is that the profession has partly lost its sense of purpose. Modern nurses are often highly skilled in a way that mirrors the modern physician. They are increasingly looking for autonomy and professional status and no longer as keen to perform the menial tasks that their sisters of the past formed in the early, often religious, schools of nursing, undertook for the glory of God. But oblivious to the values of this school of thought, they alienate themselves from the origins of their profession. According to Ann Bradshaw, nursing provides an example of the kind of moral crisis that Alasdair MacIntyre has identified within our post-Enlightenment society. It is characterized by fragmented values, on the ba-

5

sis of which it is difficult to find "moral reasons to submit oneself to the service of people who are strangers, and who may at times seem unattractive, unappreciative, difficult, and even dangerous, giving the kind of self-denying and compassionate service of washing, cleaning, holding, that being a nurse involves." And so Ann Bradshaw calls for a renewal of the spirit of this tradition in order to foster the ethos of care that must remain the core of nursing.

Of course, this kind of renewal and adherence to the values of the nursing tradition will require a firm faith. Thus Arlene Miller in her chapter, "Communicating Christian Conviction: Ethics of spiritual care," discusses nurses' responsibility when their Christian spirituality and the patient's spirituality meet. Explaining the need for and nature of spiritual care in nursing, she argues that professional nurses do not necessarily face ethical problems when they engage in spiritual care from a Christian perspective. Taking into account the patient's needs and context, nurses can both respectfully and adequately provide spiritual care.

2.2 Moral tensions in specific relationships

Taking for granted the foregoing discussions of nursing as a Christian practice of care, Kees Kleingeld in his chapter, "Professional Responsibility in the Patient-Nurse Relationship," examines the extent to which the patient's responsibility for his own health has a bearing on nurses' professional responsibility. In so doing, he discusses the following nursing models: the mother model, the contract model, and different versions of the patient advocate model. He finds them all more or less wanting. The mother and contract models allow little room for the patient's own responsibility, while the advocacy model entails too limited a view of nurses' responsibility. Kees Kleingeld therefore suggests an alternative understanding of the relationship, one that does not deny the role of moral advocate but centers on nursing care as a means of helping the patient to "overcome or alleviate the consequences of illness, handicap, or medical treatment."

Turning from the nurse-patient relationship to that between nurses, Fu-Jin Shih in her chapter, "Professional Responsibility in Nurses' Relationships to Colleagues and Their Profession," argues that an important role for Christian nurses is that of peacemaker or mediator in times of conflict involving nursing colleagues. Looking at a number of situations in which nurses may disagree about what is best for the patient and suggesting ways of handling these situations, she stresses the importance of a respectful attitude towards others and a willingness to seek to understand the views and beliefs of colleagues and patients from different cultures. Only then is it possible to promote good working relationships between colleagues and also promote good nursing care for patients.

The chapter by Jan van der Wolf, "Professional Responsibility in Health Care Teams and Cooperative Working Relationships," complements the preceding two by dealing with the relationship between nurses and colleagues in other health care professions. Van der Wolf is more concerned with how nurses can foster good working relationships in general, rather than how they act as mediators in conflict situations. Speaking about the social skills of nurses, and especially of the Christian nurse, he emphasizes courage to speak up and compassion for patients. Nurses should recognize that because their responsibilities differ from those of doctors, their role should be that of co-worker rather than assistant.

2.3 Moral tensions in specific situations

Following these three chapters on nurses' responsibilities to patients, and relationships with colleagues and other health care professions, Ada van Bruchem-Van de Scheur in her chapter, "Professional Responsibility at the End of Life: Euthanasia and palliative care," deals with the problems facing nurses confronted by requests for euthanasia. Her chapter is clearly of relevance for nurses in the Netherlands and Belgium, where euthanasia is legal, and for nurses in the State of Oregon, where physician-assisted suicide is legal. However, with increasing demands for euthanasia elsewhere, her argument concerns us all. She explains that no part of nurses' professional responsibility calls for participation in the execution of euthanasia, because "it runs counter to the principles of her professional responsibility." Generally relevant, too, is her understanding of good palliative care. She argues that the incurably ill need medical as well as social and spiritual care, even though the medical attention required would not be aimed at curing but at alleviating pain and other unpleasant physical symptoms. Good palliative care, she argues, aims at providing optimal total patient care not least for the terminally ill. And here, she says, nurses' roles are crucial. They must not shrink from their responsibility to insist on being party to any decisions made about their patients.

The next chapter, Dónal O'Mathúna's "Professional Responsibility Concerning Alternative Therapies," calls for prudence in using alternative therapies, especially on the part of Christian nurses. Certain alternative therapies involve the occult realm, which Judeo-Christian teaching has always viewed as dangerous. If, as has been pointed out in many of the chapters in this book, the primary responsibility of nurses is the provision of nursing caring, a second recognized responsibility is that of provision of knowledge-based information, O'Mathúna argues. Therefore, Christian nurses have a special responsibility to warn patients about certain forms of alternative therapies, on the grounds that they involve occult forces.

The closing chapter for this volume, "Professional Responsibility Regarding Intimacy and Sexuality in Patient Care," is by Bart Cusveller and

7

Dónal O'Mathúna. This explores how nurses, and in particular Christian nurses, might cope with the sexuality of patients, especially in situations involving intimate care or care of the mentally handicapped. Arguing for respect for personal integrity, bodily as well as spiritual, they show that different situations invite different degrees of intimacy and that it is important for nurses to be sensitive and not overstep the proper limits. They also point out that no part of nurses' responsibility involves helping patients in their pursuit of sexual activities. Most nursing codes explicitly rule out sexual relationships between nurses and patients and argue that such relationships would hinder rather than promote a healing nurse-patient relationship. Here, as in the other chapters, Christian nurses are encouraged to bear witness to their faith and convictions.

3. Terminology
3.1 Ethics and morals
A few words on how terminology is used in this book will help nurses who are less familiar with ethical approaches in nursing. A natural place to start are the adjectives "ethical" and "moral" and their counterparts "ethics" and "morals" (or "morality"). Even though these terms can often be used interchangeably, it could be argued that *ethics* is the reflection (theoretical or otherwise) on morality. *Morality* in turn pertains to the praise- and blame-worthiness of human behavior. What makes behavior praise- or blameworthy (morally right or wrong) is a point of debate among ethicists. Some believe that morality is little more than social convention, or power arrangements, or residual emotions. Therefore, we must come clean right at the beginning. The authors of these essays adhere to the view that morality has to do with human *flourishing*, i.e., the way they are meant to live. They also believe that human beings can know what are right and wrong ways to live. To some degree, all humans know intuitively about right and wrong, but it is especially through a prayerful life with God's Holy Spirit and his Holy Scripture that humans can learn how they are meant to live. If Christian nurses are to make full-fledged moral judgments, then they are to use everything they know, including what they know as Christians.

3.2 Conflicts, dilemmas and tensions
In this collection, there will also be much talk of moral problems, conflicts, dilemmas, and tensions. The way these terms will be used flows from our understanding of the concepts of moral norms and values. These latter concepts have also been much debated. To make our perspective explicit

here as well, we take the concept of (moral) *value* to coincide with the goods human beings are due in order to flourish. These are valuable states of affairs because they make a difference for the good life. Moral *norms* on the other hand are the standards or rules that we uphold in our conduct with an eye to achieving those values or goods. One reason to uphold the norm not to lie, for example, is that the values of being trustworthy and honest is presented to us (e.g. by Scripture) as elements of the good life, obeying God's word and honoring his character.

Now, if something or someone hinders us in our efforts to achieve something good, we have a moral problem on our hands: something of moral value is not achieved. Sometimes, the achievement of one moral value is incompatible with another moral value (or even a nonmoral value). For instance, we really would like the patient to quit smoking, but his autonomy has to be respected. Then we have a moral *conflict*. Sometimes, both moral values are about as important to us and we simply have to choose one of them. Imagine a case where telling the truth to a terminal patient seems equally important as respecting his peace of mind. Then we have a moral *dilemma*. Sometimes, furthermore, a choice is not difficult, but it may still be difficult to see how we should exactly perform the moral act. Suppose it is good to tell a patient the truth about his prognosis; still, when, where, and how to go about telling him will make a big difference to the moral quality of the interaction. We could speak of a moral *tension*. The whole of these conflicts, dilemmas, and tensions we group together as moral *problems*.

3.3 Moral and other responsibilities

There are many other important concepts in the realm of ethics and morality, such as rights, justice, and virtue. We cannot explain them all and do not have to for the purposes of this book. One more concept that is of central importance to this book, however, is the idea of moral responsibility. As there will be an entire chapter on this notion, we need not focus extensively on it here. But it will be helpful to delineate it from other notions pertinent to nursing practice.

As we have seen, morality is a matter of human flourishing. It will be clear that there can be no human flourishing without community with other persons, including God. So there will be interaction among human beings about what they are due and, since we believe morality can be really binding on people (since our highest moral authority is Divine), expectations and requirements may have the force of a *duty*. But the relational nature of human life and morality means that duties have a social aspect as well: they are binding; moral expectations one person has of another. Persons, further-more, may hold each other *accountable* for living up to their duties, to the expectations and requirements involved. This twofold notion of moral duty and moral accountability we call moral *responsibility*. With the notion of moral responsibility before us, we can delineate it from other forms of re-sponsibility. There is political responsibility: for instance, the Minister of Health can see her political responsibility to require that she resign, perhaps without having flouted any moral responsibility. Equally, we can speak of legal, social, and maybe even causal responsibility, without implying moral responsibility. Hence, it is conceivable to flout a legal responsibility without flouting any moral responsibility, or vice versa, to flout moral responsibility without flouting legal (or political or social) responsibility. In this volume, the focus is on moral responsibility alone even though in nursing this will ordinarily be entangled with social and legal responsibilities.

4. Conclusion

The idea for this book originated from a group of authors who wrote a book for the Prof.dr. G.A. Lindeboom Instituut in Ede, The Netherlands. It was in response to what they saw as a need for discernment among Chris-tian nurses in a secular environment. The original Dutch volume is now being used as a textbook in Christian nursing programs and was critically acclaimed by professional journals. In 1999, it won the annual award for Christian contributions to social work and health care from the Reformed University for Higher Professional Education in Zwolle, The Netherlands (the "GH Prize"). This positive reception prompted the vision that an in-ternational audience of Christian nurses might also profit from an adapta-tion of this original book. The present volume is the fruit of that vision.

This book articulates an understanding of nursing as a profession and practice shaped by the tradition of Christian values. The authors' goal is to promote patient care that respects the dignity and life of each and every patient. In so doing, we encourage Christian nurses to remain true to their Christian tradition by bearing witness to it in both word and action. Thus, the aim is to fill a lacuna in the nursing ethics literature, since many works in this field, like in medical ethics, are written from a secular point of view. Indeed, we are directing ourselves not only at Christian readers but also at nonchristian ones, offering our understanding of nurses' professional re-sponsibilities as they encounter ethical problems in practicing their profes-sion. But above all, we are seeking to provide the tools and attitudes that Christian nurses need to engage in debate and dialogue with the world around them.

10

2

What is Professional Responsibility in Nursing Practice?

Bart Cusveller

Vignette

Little Esther, age 3, is admitted to the pediatric ward of a general hospital for observation of unspecified stomach aches. The ward allows for so-called "rooming in," i.e., parents are allowed to spend the night in the vicinity of their child's bed. Making her first round of her night shift, Nurse Sue discovers the railings of Esther's bed have not been secured. Fortunately, Esther did not tumble out of bed during that time, but she might very well have done so. Suppose an accident had occurred? This situation makes Sue wonder what exactly the parent's responsibility was and what exactly the nurse's responsibility was.

1. Introduction

This chapter explores the central concept of this book, namely the concept of professional responsibility. My contention is that the concept of professional responsibility helps us understand and tackle moral problems in nursing practice. Also, it is my belief that the concept provides common ground for Christian nurses and other health care professionals to discuss moral problems openly. I will now proceed to substantiate these statements.

Christian nurses are members of two communities: the community of Christians and the community of nurses. Each community has its distinct goals, rules, doctrines, schooling, practices, and so on. Christian nurses have accepted the responsibility to professionally provide care for the weak, the sick, and the suffering. Thus they accept their professional responsibility, to an important degree, as consistent with their Christian responsibility (or they would not join the profession). We should not assume, however, that professional responsibility and Christian responsibility always coincide. Not all professional goals, beliefs, or practices of nursing are compatible with or overlap with those of a Christian life. This may even be truer today than at any other time. Christian nurses may sometimes want to improve existing nursing practice when certain aspects of it are not in accordance with their Christian commitment.[1] In other words, they may at times want to promote an understanding of their professional responsibility that is determined by their Christian perspective.

So we ask, are the responsibilities of Christian nurses congruent with those of their profession?[2] To be a Christian in today's world of nursing, Christian nurses need an account of their professional responsibility that is faithful to their Christian commitment. Of course, Christian nurses may argue that, say, a patient's request for mercy killing or certain alternative therapies is not compatible with their responsibilities as Christians. It is sometimes necessary to refuse to provide certain types of care, even if legally permitted. But such responses, often based on theological arguments, may lead to Christian nurses resorting to conscientious objection arguments and having themselves removed from caring for such patients altogether.

We need to avoid situations where Christian nurses *refuse* to care for those patients; the point is rather how *best* to care for them. If Christians object to providing certain types of care (euthanasia, say), they should not withdraw from the situation entirely and let others step in. In this situation, their objection is really that *no one* should provide such care. Their argument is not only that such care cannot be a part of their Christian responsibility, but that such care is bad practice. And bad practice can neither be part of their Christian responsibility nor of their professional responsibility. In that case, they should have a professional argument which they should use to improve (or prevent deterioration in) patient care. Here, then, they will need an account of where their professional responsibility is congruent with their Christian responsibility to help them understand and deal with certain moral problems in patient care.

---

[1] Some of those points will be explored more fully in following chapters of this book.

[2] Cusveller, B.S. "Does Being a Christian Make a Difference?" *Christian Nurse International* 15.2 (1999): 4-6.

In this chapter I sketch a Christian account of nurses' professional responsibility. First I will explore the concept of responsibility within a Christian framework, then that of *professional* responsibility, and lastly that of *nurses'* professional responsibility. This discussion will require a small injection of moral philosophy, but it won't hurt.[3]

2. Responsibility
2.1. Obligation and answerability
Fundamentally, I take responsibility to be a normative trait ascribed to human agents such as nurses, requiring two inseparable things:[4]

- An obligation. One is responsible for something or someone; some state of affairs has to be brought about. Call this the "content" of responsibility;
- Answerability. One is responsible to something or someone. Responsibility entails an obligation or duty as well as a requirement to answer for the performance of that obligation of duty. Call this the "source" of responsibility.[5]

What has to be done (or the something or someone that one is responsible for) depends on several things, such as one's situation and one's abilities. If I have no children, I can have no responsibility to care for them. If I have, I have responsibilities to care for them, even if those change as they age. If I have poor health, this condition may indicate that I do not have a responsibility to become a missionary in the tropics. However, one's responsibility also depends on the something or someone one is accountable to, and so by what or whom one is held responsible. In other words, people are made responsible—or given responsibility—by something or someone. For obeying the professional code of conduct, say, I may be held responsible by (representatives of) my profession. For bringing back the car in one piece, I am held responsible by the owner. The content of my responsibility, then, depends in an important way on its source, i.e., the something or someone holding me responsible, or to what or whom I am accountable. What is required of me depends, in other words, on where the requirement comes from, on what or who gives me responsibility.

---

[3] I will not be discussing e.g. the legal side of professional responsibility (accountability), or the theological side of Christian responsibility. For the latter, see Shelly, J.A. and Miller, A.B. *Called to Care: A Christian theology of nursing.* Downers Grove: InterVarsity, 1999.

[4] Cole, G.A. "Responsibility." *New Dictionary of Christian Ethics and Pastoral Theology.* Eds. Atkinson, D.J. and Field, D.H. Leicester/Downers Grove: InterVarsity, 1995. 734-736.

[5] Schweiker, W. *Responsibility and Christian Ethics.* Cambridge: Cambridge University, 1995. 55; cf. 74.

This source of responsibility I will call *authority*, in the sense of having a legitimate claim over someone. A profession has a certain authority over its members regarding their conduct (say, a legitimate claim to the payment of membership fees); the owner has a certain authority over my use of his car (a legitimate claim to its careful use). That kind of authority gives us specific responsibility and requires us to do certain things and account for what we do or fail to do.

2.2 Authority

So let us start our discussion of the professional responsibility of the nurse with a discussion of the source of responsibility, i.e., authority. To whom do nurses answer? It will be helpful to distinguish between "areas" or "levels" of authority.[6] The best way of doing so is, perhaps, negatively. Some responsibilities may conflict, as we all know. My responsibilities as a father and a husband are not always in concordance with my responsibility as an employee, as is the case when I stay late at work, for instance. In such situations we usually find, however, that certain responsibilities outweigh or override others. In the case where my responsibility as a father suffers from those as an employee, I am usually justified in readjusting the situation by giving precedence to the former over the latter. Why? Because in that situation my family usually has a stronger legitimate claim on me–and in that sense a higher level of authority–than my employer has. In other respects, however, my employer retains a certain area or level of authority over me.

Given different levels of authority, we may wonder who or what has the highest level of authority in human existence. What is the final source of our being responsible? For Christians, the answer is clear: it is the Lord God, who speaks to us in Scripture and through the Holy Spirit. Because He is the highest authority, we are ultimately responsible to Him. We are *called*–called to be free, says the Apostle, free from bondage by sin and free to obey only Christ, but called nonetheless. Discussing the sources, levels, and contents of responsibility, I conclude that the acceptance of moral responsibility in the end involves a religious commitment, something that makes people live out that responsibility. Likewise, nurses' professional responsibility ultimately involves a religious commitment. In discussing the content of professional responsibility, Christian nurses are ultimately led to the question: What is it that God requires me to do and to answer for in nursing?

---

[6] Cf. Kilner, J. *Life on the Line. Ethics, Aging, Ending Patient's Lives, and Allocation Vital Resources.* Grand Rapids: Eerdmans, 1992. Ch. 3, esp. 65-69.

2.3 Care

To determine what nurses are ultimately held responsible for and by whom requires reflection on the place of care in human existence. For care is the thing that they are expected to show and provide. In brief, God created us in His image to live harmoniously in relationship or communion with Him, with ourselves, and with our fellow human beings. He also created us so that we would live in harmonious relationships with Him, with others, with nature, and with ourselves. In short, we are created to live in shalom.[7] In doing so, God "graced" us with responsibilities. To be sure, human life does not solely consist in having responsibilities—we also have rights and, further, we rightly enjoy and celebrate God's gifts. But when God created us he placed us under the requirement to preserve and cultivate creation, including preserving and cultivating the human community as a good thing in itself; He has the right to ask what we have done to live up to that requirement (Genesis 1:28, 2:15).[8]

Living as human beings, therefore, means to flourish in community with the responsibility to support one another's capacities to similarly flourish, e.g. to help and care for the young and the elderly, to honor their place in the human community. The Bible calls such living in shalom "healthy." Health or total well-being, then, is the capacity to live as we were created to live, i.e., to have "the power to live as human beings."[9] And since we have a responsibility to help each other to live thus, we have a responsibility to look after each other's well-being. This mutual concern, I propose, is the role of care in human existence. Note that I interpret this role from a specific worldview. I fail to see how it could be otherwise.

Sadly, we must add immediately that things (and people) have not stayed the way God created them. Creation was, and continues to be, compromised by sin, our turning away from God. What concerns us here, primarily, is that sin distorts our capacities to live in harmonious community with each other and with God. Sin interferes with health; it causes suffering and death. Because this reality should not be so, human beings are left with the responsibility to support the suffering and the dying as best as possible. Care is not limited to preservation and cultivation of the creation but includes the responsibility to restore and mitigate the vulnerability and suffering in the

---

[7] Shelly and Miller 2000, 167 ff.

[8] Bouma, H. et al. *Health, Christian Faith, and Medical Practice.* Grand Rapids: Eerdmans, 1989. Chs. 1 and 2, esp. 27-34.

[9] Barth, K. excerpt from *Church Dogmatics* III/4. Cited in *On Moral Medicine. Theological perspectives in medical ethics.* Eds. Lammers, S.E. and Verhey, A. Grand Rapids: Eerdmans, 1987. 6-10.

fallen human condition. We do so because we believe this is not a hopeless undertaking. For God did not leave us in the mires of our misery but sent His Son Jesus Christ to restore the relationship between God, people, and creation. Assuming responsibility for each other, then, looking after each other's capacities to flourish as humans, is to take on the responsibility to follow Christ's example and instructions, to assume the responsibility to bear witness to His redemptive work, and to assume the responsibility to make visible something of the human flourishing that lies ahead of us in His coming Kingdom. Care is working toward shalom, even in this distorted existence. We are both created and destined to live in shalom (Revelation 21:3-4).

In short, life as full-fledged human beings does not just happen to us as we mature. We need to work to promote it and take care of it. We humans have a responsibility to support each other's ability to live as we are supposed to, to look after each other's well-being. Sometimes we can take care of ourselves. Sometimes, we need each other's assistance. Our responsibility to care for others increases as their capacities to care for themselves and others decreases. To be sure, each human being retains responsibility to care for his or her own well-being, not just because of the instrumental value for preserving the well-being of others, but more so for the intrinsic value the well-being of a human person itself has.[10] That's what makes caring *ethical.*

3. Helping and caring as a professional responsibility

3.1 Professional care

So far, I have argued that responsibility is central to care, and that care is central to human existence. We turn now to the concept of care as professional responsibility. Care can be difficult, unpleasant, time-consuming, and wearisome. Living with a handicapped child is not easy; supporting a dying relative can be exhausting; helping someone with a rare condition may require specific knowledge and skills. In such cases we ordinarily do our best, but unfortunately sometimes more needs to be done.

Consequently, we often have to call upon the help of people who have the required knowledge, skills, resources, and endurance. These people may even have made it their occupation to give that kind of help or care, as is often the case in our modern, western society. We call upon a group of people who—we trust—are able and prepared to give the kind of care that is more than we can usually give. These people, such as nurses, are able and

---

[10] Puolimatka, T. *Moral Realism and Justification.* Helsinki: Finnish Academy of Science and Letters, 1989. 143.

prepared to carry (part of) the responsibility that we cannot carry ourselves. Note that since religious belief commits some people to certain responsibilities and to certain sources of responsibility, faith may commit some people to become members of this group of "helping people."

These people are usually organized as a group, rather than operating as individuals. In that way, they can organize their training, their resources, their level of quality (by supervision, nursing audit, etc.), and their powers of endurance. For instance, as a group they can endure difficult work by sharing tasks and taking turns to take a break, go home, have a holiday, et cetera. They assume the responsibility to care for other people's well-being collectively. So, when I go to a hospital, I do not call upon some individual I happen to know, but upon members of an organized group of people who look after me in turn. This is also why nurses (and their employers) would have been held accountable should little Esther in our vignette at the beginning of the chapter have fallen out of her bed.

As a group, in addition, these people monitor each other's ability, motivation, willingness, or commitment to accept the responsibility to care for those who ask for help. This accountability is the reason that (in many countries) they take an oath or pledge of sorts after completing their training and before entering the practice. They solemnly promise in public to use their knowledge and skills to serve the well-being of those who call upon them, whatever benefits they themselves may gain. In other words, they *profess* to assume the responsibility for the well-being of others in need. That commitment is why they are called members of a *profession*–"professionals." That is the reason, moreover, why trust is so important in the relationship between health care professionals and patients. People in need must rely on people who promise to help.[11]

3.2 The core of care

Given this source of professional responsibility in health care, we could formulate its content as fostering the well-being of patients to the best of one's ability.[12] We add emphatically that health care workers promote other people's well-being *for its own sake*, as a good thing in itself, not just as in-

---

[11] Cf. Koehn, D. *The Ground of Professional Ethics*. London: Routledge, 1994. 56-59; Gastmans, C., Dierckx de Casterle, C. and Schotsmans, P. "Nursing Considered as Moral Practice: A philosophical-ethical interpretation of nursing." *Kennedy Institute of Ethics Journal* 8.1 (1998): 43-69; Cooper, M.C. "Covenantal Relationships: Grounding for the nursing ethic." *Advances in Nursing Science* 10:4 (1988): 48-59.

[12] Bishop, A.H. and Scudder, J.D. *The Practical, Moral and Personal Sense of Nursing*. Albany: SUNY, 1990. 171.

strumentally valuable, i.e., as professionals they are to help the *patient*. As individuals, professionals may have other motivations for doing their work, such as spreading the gospel, earning a living, or achieving a sense of satisfaction. However laudable these other intentions, the central value of nursing work is to help others. As professionals, nurses promote the patient's well-being for the good of the patient, not for their own betterment. In this sense, their type of work is disinterested, unselfish. They may be unselfish themselves, too. But then again they may not. I think they are likely to last longer in nursing, however, if they are unselfish in this sense. They have to be "cut from the right wood."[13] Here, their religious commitment informs their acceptance and understanding of the responsibility to pursue the central value of their profession. (Perhaps this commitment need not necessarily be Christian. As long as it is consistent with the central value of nursing care, it need not bother Christians whether the commitment of colleagues is Christian.)

If the well-being of patients is a moral value (because they are created by and in the image of God), fostering it is a moral practice. And if this is the professional responsibility of health care workers, their professional responsibility is ultimately a moral responsibility. As Jesus suggested to the Pharisees regarding the Sabbath, curing someone is not merely work, it is rescuing him (Luke 14:2-5). We therefore take issue with the line of thought that views the responsibility of health care professionals primarily as applying theoretical knowledge, following technical procedure, obeying law and contract, or rendering service for fee. The idea of care is to help people, regardless of whether it also involves theory, technology, contract, or fee.[14] It is the health care professionals' responsibility to understand and pursue this central value as well as possible. Consequently, the term "professional" should not be used to signify merely what is based on evidence or research or the like, but to signify what contributes most to the moral purpose of caring practices. This alone makes it indispensable for nurses to study ethics, the moral tradition of care,[15] and the religious tradition issuing the values and norms of nursing care.[16]

---

[13] Cusveller, B.S. "Cut From the Right Wood: Spirituality and pluralism in professional nursing practice." *Journal of Advanced Nursing* 28:2 (1998): 266-273.

[14] Cusveller, B.S. "A View From Somewhere: The presence and function of religious commitment in nursing practice." *Journal of Advanced Nursing* 22:5 (1995): 973-978.

[15] Edgar, A. "Nursing as a Moral Tradition." *Journal of Advances in Health and Nursing Care* 2.1 (1993): 3-20.

[16] Bradshaw, A. *Lighting the Lamp: The spiritual dimension of nursing care.* London: Scutari, 1994. Esp. Ch. 2.

4. Nurses' professional responsibility

Up to this point I have spoken of the source and content of nurses' professional responsibility, narrowing the focus from the general human responsibility to care down to the specific professional responsibility of health care workers. Yet, nurses are a particular kind of health care worker, and I have not made any attempt to delineate their specific professional responsibility. After all, within that larger responsibility of fostering the patient's well-being, doctors and nurses do have different professional responsibilities. So, we must say something about the professional responsibility specific to nurses.

In order to distinguish the responsibility of medicine from that of nursing, I differentiate between their respective central values. As we have seen, health care professionals are to promote the well-being of people who are finding it difficult to assume the responsibility of caring for themselves and others. In other words, they are to care for people whose ability to live as human beings is not fully realized. Or to use different terminology, their ability to undertake the activities of daily living (taken broadly) is diminished. One way to state the difference between the professional responsibilities of doctors and nurses, then, is as follows. The physician's primary responsibility is to attend to the particular disorders or pathological processes that affect the patient's daily activities necessary for human life. For instance, he treats the fractured bone in someone's broken wrist. The nurse's primary responsibility is to attend to the effects of those disorders on the patient's daily activities. For instance, the nurse helps someone recovering from a broken wrist to eat. It remains the patient's own responsibility to decide what daily activities to engage in or not. For instance, he is responsible himself for deciding to drink either milk or a double whisky.

Certainly, promoting the patient's well-being is part of the general responsibility of every health care professional (and maybe of every human being). Consequently, sometimes nurses must assume a share of the responsibility normally allotted to some other health care professional, like the physician (however differently this may be arranged legally or practically in different countries). So there can be both conflict and cooperation between the health care professions.

We are now in a position to see what help a Christian account of professional responsibility offers in understanding and resolving moral problems in nursing care. Since the central value of nursing care (attending to the well-being of a patient in the specific nursing way) is a moral value, everything that obstructs its achievement (which is nurses' professional responsibility) creates a moral dilemma. Rooted in the inherent dignity invested in

19

human life by God's creation, necessitated by the ravaging effects of the fall, called by the promise of God's shalom in Jesus Christ, the Christian nurse sees an ethical dilemma where circumstances obstruct fostering patients' well-being and health.

There are two types of such dilemmas. The first is the type where the fulfillment of the professional responsibility of nursing is frustrated by the pursuit of another moral value. For example, the mental well-being of a dying patient has to be weighed against speaking the truth about his condition. The moral value of love or caring then competes with the moral value of truthfulness. The other type of moral dilemma arises when the promotion of the patient's well-being is frustrated by a nonmoral value. Such an issue may occur when the well-being of a patient has to be weighed against, say, efficiency in the use of time and resources available to nurses (which is a value, but not *per se* a moral value). Both types, I hold, are truly moral dilemmas for nurses since they involve their moral responsibility and are inherent to their practice.[17]

Although nursing's central value is a moral value, it needs mentioning that *everything* in nursing is not *per se* moral (nor is every dilemma in nursing a moral dilemma). Seldom (if ever) does one promote a patient's well-being by just one intervention. Usually, one must perform several tasks with that aim and to the best of one's ability. Some ways, then, are better than others. In other words, practicing a profession consists in interventions and presence which respect various norms. These norms stipulate to what extent the interventions and presence promote the end of the practice. But these norms (such as the requirement to be hygienic) are in themselves not necessarily all moral norms. Instead, they may be of a technological, scientific, economic, legal, or social nature. Technical problems call for technical solutions. Every nurse learns how to cope with certain techniques, which interventions have been proven by research to be better than others, which methods are economically more prudent than others, which actions are legally excluded or included in proper care, which ways of treating a patient are socially acceptable and which are not. This is why not everything in nursing is immediately decided on moral grounds, so that not every dilemma is a moral dilemma. Nevertheless, to uphold those norms is a professional responsibility for nurses, in as far as they serve to promote the patient's well-being and health.

---

[17] As is brilliantly demonstrated by Chambliss, D.F. *Beyond Caring: Hospitals, nurses, and the social organization of ethics.* Chicago: University of Chicago, 1996.

One last–and maybe most important–point regarding nursing's professional responsibility. Nurses sometimes cannot do what their professional responsibility requires (leading to moral dilemmas), but sometimes nurses are asked to do things that do not belong within their professional responsibility. In my own country for instance, nurses are invited to assist in euthanasia. This, I suggest, is not an ethical dilemma, although most nurses would feel that it is one. Rather, assistance in euthanasia is simply not part of their professional responsibility, as has been confirmed legally, even in the Netherlands. The proper response of nurses is not that they have moral or religious or conscientious objections to euthanasia, although they may have them and use them ("the theological arguments"); the proper response is that their professional responsibility is to provide optimal care for a dying patient which nowhere entails helping to end that patient's life. They need not take recourse to a minority position: they can appeal to the central value of their profession (a "professional argument").

5. Conclusion

Several professional responsibilities were spoken of above, along with various ways in which religious commitment is involved. To summarize, the primary professional responsibility of nurses is the following: *To foster to the best of their ability the intrinsic value of the well-being of patients by attending to the effects health disorders have on patients' ability to perform activities of daily living.* This mission involves the following (secondary) responsibilities:

- to maintain skills and knowledge to do so,
- to uphold the several norms that specify professional ways to do so,
- to improve skills, knowledge, methods, and norms,
- to maintain certain necessary conditions for patient care,
- to support other health care workers,
- to contribute to the formation of novices.

Furthermore, Christian commitment to nursing practice involves these elements:

- acceptance of the responsibility to care for others (compassion),
- motivation to enter the profession (calling),
- understanding and acceptance of the responsibility to foster the central value of the profession (dedication),
- understanding, acceptance, and promotion of the responsibility to uphold norms (competence).

If nursing practice has historically been intertwined with Christian faith in this inextricable way, could it not be so today and in the future? I conclude that it is possible, relevant, and legitimate for Christian nurses to develop their account of professional responsibility and voice it in nursing practice when faced with moral problems.

In the remainder of this book we will look in more detail at some specific areas of moral problems: the relationships with patients, nurses, and other health care professionals, as well as the situations of religious diversity, end-of-life decisions, sexuality and intimacy, and alternative therapies. The general strategy of these chapters will be, first, to locate the professional responsibility of nurses in the context under consideration; second, to identify the moral problems that may be expected to arise in this area; and third, to answer the question of how the Christian nurse is to deal with those problems, given her professional responsibility.

Acknowledgement

The author extends his gratitude to Christian nursing scholars at the NCFI conferences in Langensteinbacherhohe (Germany, 1998) and Edinburgh (Scotland, 2000) for valuable interaction, and notably to Tove Giske of Bergen, Norway, for extensive written comments.

Discussion questions

1. Does Nurse Sue, in the vignette of this chapter, have a responsibility to check little Esther's bed railings, even when Esther's parents are available? Why or why not?

2. Suppose Esther was a grown woman and her children came to visit her. Would nurse Sue's responsibility for Esther's safety be any different? Why or why not?

3. How should Sue try to determine her responsibility? What could she do once she becomes more informed?

4. Do you think her responsibility as a nurse, as a Christian, and as a human being are three separate things? Why or why not?

5. Which norms, values, and responsibilities would Sue find in her profession's codes of conduct, codes of ethics, and national policy statements that would help in this sort of situation? How do they compare with a Christian understanding of her professional responsibility?

3

Changing Perceptions of Nurses' Professional Responsibility and Lessons from History

A view from the United Kingdom

Ann Bradshaw

Vignette

Jane Smith, a recently registered nurse, arrived on the ward for an early shift. The nursing student she was mentoring, Paul, arrived at the same time. Even before Jane had received the night report she heard a patient's call bell sounding its raucous and impatient summons. One of the registered nurses passed Jane and Paul and muttered "Oh, that's Mr. Brown again. He never stopped ringing his bell all night!"

Jane knew Mr. Brown, a man of 80, who had been in the ward for many weeks awaiting placement in a nursing home. He was not seriously ill, but he was lonely and unhappy because he could no longer care for himself, and he had become incontinent. Jane asked Paul to come with her, and they went to Mr. Brown. "Can we help you?" she asked quietly. "Yes, you can!" muttered Mr. Brown angrily. "I've been lying here for hours and no one has come to me. I am thirsty, and my bed feels uncomfortable."

As she stifled her own irritation, knowing how much there was to do, Jane said she would look at the bed. As she lifted the sheet Jane saw the bed was soiled and she thought she also saw a pressure sore on Mr. Brown's hip. How should Jane respond professionally to Mr. Brown, and what should she teach Paul about their proper priorities and attitude in this situation? What relevance has nursing history to guide Jane in her response?

1. Introduction

In 1986, the editor of the *Journal of Medical Ethics*, Raanan Gillon, raised some important questions about the direction of nursing ethics.[1] In a response to Jenifer Wilson-Barnett, an eminent British professor of nursing,[2] who argued that there were benefits for patients if nurses become more independent in their ethical decision making, Gillon questioned some of her basic assumptions. In addition to issues of patient welfare and nurses' individual moral autonomy, Gillon argued, Wilson-Barnett's article pointed to a third strand of contemporary nursing concern, the desire to shed the handmaiden role and find a niche as an independent profession, complementary rather than ancillary to medicine. Gillon sought to challenge the view that nursing professionalization and independence were necessarily beneficial for patients:

> Many of the traditional "handmaiden" tasks which nurses perform are essential for patients' welfare but do not obviously require professional status. Comforting, chatting with, holding hands with, stroking, feeding, grooming, washing, bathing, cleaning, and making beds for other people when they are sick are all traditional nursing tasks, and in many circumstances essential for patient care. But do they require professional skills or professional autonomy to be carried out effectively? Or is there some reason to expect that professionals are likely to reject many such tasks as inappropriate to their status and a waste of their expensive professional time and skills?[3]

Even the hallowed guarding and distribution of drugs by nurses in the hospital, Gillon argued, hardly required professional skills. After all, patients are self-medicating when they get home, he suggested, and therefore "[it] seems more a matter of providing a simple service to those patients who are sick enough to need it."[4]

---

[1] Gillon, R. "Nursing Ethics and Medical Ethics." [editorial] *Journal of Medical Ethics* 12.3 (1986): 115-116, 122.

[2] Wilson-Barnett, J. "Ethical Dilemmas in Nursing." *Journal of Medical Ethics* 12 (1986): 123-126,135.

[3] Gillon 1986, 116.

[4] Gillon 1986, 116.

On the other hand, Gillon thought, it could be argued that even these skills can be handled in a professional way. Nursing could acquire a vast array of additional skills mirroring the new skills acquired by medicine. Nurses could specialize in psychological counseling, high-technology intensive care, chemotherapy, independent care for the dying, general practice and nurse-practitioner work, hospital management, occupational health, or traditional specialties such as surgery, midwifery, and district nursing. All these specialties involved nurses in the more or less independent exercise of special skills.

Gillon argued that, given this wide range of functions, it is difficult to see how nurses could find a single solution to their dilemmas over occupational status, and while he appreciated the concern for status and occupational self-interest, he thought it important that this was distinguished from two other motives of concern with professional ethics, namely protection of the patients' interests and respect for the moral agency of individual nurses:

> The obvious danger if nurses fail to keep distinct the three components of their developing concern with professional ethics is that patients will suffer as, in the name of nursing ethics, they are used as shuttlecocks in an increasingly bitter interprofessional battle about the occupational status of nursing. That is an outcome which all who are concerned with the welfare of patients would surely wish to avoid.[5]

Gillon's editorial focuses the debate on nurses' professional responsibility in the context of a changing UK nursing profession. His analysis reflects a deep uneasiness about the changing role and responsibility of the nurse that was occurring at the end of the twentieth century. The changes began in the early 1970s, in the face of much grass-root nursing opinion, and made the profession into "new nursing."[6] The nursing profession was remade on a new basis. By the late twentieth-century the role and purpose of the "new nurse" had become increasingly unclear: On the one hand, the health care assistant and nursing auxiliary were taking over what was previously thought of as "hands-on" nursing work and even more invasive procedures;[7] while on the other hand, nurses were expanding their role to include work traditionally done by doctors.[8]

---

[5] Gillon 1986, 122.

[6] Salvage, J. "The Theory and Practice of the 'New Nursing.'" [Occasional Paper] *Nursing Times* 86.4 (January 24, 1990): 42-45.

[7] Thornley, C. *The Invisible Workers: An investigation into the pay and employment of health care assistants in the NHS.* London: Unison Health Care, 1997; Thornley, C. *Neglected Nurses, Hidden Work: An investigation into the pay and employment of nursing auxiliaries and assistants in the NHS,* London: Unison Health Care, 1998.

[8] Doyal, L. Dowling, S. and Cameron, A. *Challenging Practice: An evaluation of four innovatory nursing posts in the South-West.* Bristol, University of Bristol: Policy, 1998.

In the years that followed confusion became evident. The new form of nurse education was not producing nurses competent and fit for practice.[9] While some argued for an all-graduate and specialized profession,[10] there was recognized to be a crisis in recruiting and retaining nurses to work at the more basic grades,[11] and increasing evidence of patients being given inadequate nursing care at even basic levels.[12] Indeed, by the year 2001 the UK government was expressing serious concerns.[13] It had become clear that patients, particularly older people who were the majority of hospital patients, were not receiving adequate nursing care.

It is arguable that the changes in the nursing role and responsibility, and hence the purpose of the nurse, had some causal link with this crisis in care. For the changes in nursing were built on a quest by some in the profession for a new moral ethos, and this involved a radical revaluation of nursing values. Underpinning this whole issue of the nature, purpose, and status of British nursing is a profound change in nursing values that had occurred during the preceding decades. Nursing values traditionally founded on the idea of nursing as a moral calling were considered to be archaic and irrelevant, and women were told to shake off economically valueless and self-denying "caring."[14] No longer should nurses be "branded" with a vocation;[15] rather, nursing needed a new professional status and ethic.[16]

The values of autonomy, independence, empowerment, and assertiveness displaced the traditional nursing values of self-effacing service and vocation. And it is arguable that as the nursing role expanded, so conversely,

---

[9] Peach, L. *UKCC Education Commission Attitudinal Survey,* UKCC and BMRB International, September 1998.

[10] Council of Deans and Heads of UK University Faculties for Nursing, Midwifery and Health Visiting. *Breaking the Boundaries.* University of Manchester: Council of Deans and Heads, 1998.

[11] House of Lords Parliamentary Debates. *Unstarred Question–Nurses in the NHS,* Vol. 590, No. 168, Col. 1539, London: Stationery Office, June 16, 1998.

[12] Health Service Commissioner for England, for Scotland and for Wales. *First Report for Session 1997-8: Annual Report for 1996-97.* [Michael Buckley] London: Stationery Office, 1998; Meredith, P. and Wood, C. *The Patient's Experience of Surgery: A selective evaluation of two hospital sites: Patient satisfaction with surgery audit service.* London: Royal College of Surgeons, August, 1997.

[13] Department of Health. *The Essence of Care.* London: Department of Health, 2001; Department of Health. *Caring for Older People: A Nursing Priority.* Report by the Nursing and Midwifery Advisory Committee. London: Department of Health, 2001; Health Service Commissioner for England, for Scotland and for Wales, *First Report for Session 2001-2002: Annual Report for 2000-2001.* [Michael Buckley] London: Stationery Office, 2001.

[14] Salvage, J. *The Politics of Nursing.* London: Heinemann, 1985; Gilligan, C. "Reply to Critics." *An Ethic of Care: Feminist and interdisciplinary perspectives.* Ed. Larabee, M.J. New York: Routledge, 1993. 207-214.

[15] Brown, J.M., Kitson, A.L. and McKnight, T.J. *Challenges in Caring.* London: Chapman & Hall, 1992. 43.

[16] Wilson-Barnett 1986, 123-126, 135.

the feeding, washing, and bathing activities of care, that Gillon mentions as "simple service," and presupposes as basic to nursing, became unattractive, mundane, and menial tasks to those who resolved to make the nurse into an autonomous professional.

This analysis of the changes in UK nursing raises a central question about the nurse's professional responsibility: is the desire and willingness to undertake apparently menial activities involved in looking after people who are ill sustainable without an underlying ethic of altruistic service? Indeed, is it even a relevant question for nursing in the modern world? History may cast light on the answer.

2. The tradition of nursing

The conception of nursing as a practical moral activity of service, revived by Florence Nightingale in nineteenth century England, was ushered in by the early church in both Western and Eastern Europe and spread by religious orders and Christian philanthropy in the community. It took as its foundation the Judeo-Christian conception of care for the stranger as *agape*, embodied in the story of the Good Samaritan. It was no accident that Nightingale's revival of altruistic care, care as a covenant rather than a contract, was directly connected to the evangelical religious movements of the Victorian era.[17]

Such was the impact of this reinvigorated tradition that it affected the deeply entrenched class system of the period. At St. Bartholomew's Hospital in London, for example, nursing probationers in 1888-1890 were daughters of architects, clergymen, farmers, manufacturers, medical men, merchants, military and naval officers, solicitors, tradesmen, and stockbrokers.[18] The daughter of a Duke was working as an ordinary nurse in one of the wards.[19] By choice and inclination nurses of all classes worked with patients of all classes, cleaning, cooking, washing, and dealing with bodily fluids, ingrained dirt, and infestation. Genteel and educated upper-middle class ladies became as servants and were even paid for their training. This vocational tradition of nursing can be captured in one picture, still in use in the second half of the twentieth century, when student nurses were taught:

---

[17] Bradshaw, A. *Lighting the Lamp: The spiritual dimension of nursing care.* London: Scutari, 1994; Bradshaw, A. "Nursing and Medicine: Cooperation or conflict?" *British Medical Journal* 311 (1995) 7000, 304-305; Bradshaw, A. "Yes! There is an Ethics of Care: An answer for Peter Allmark." *Journal of Medical Ethics* 22.1 (1996): 8-12; Bradshaw, A. "Charting Some Challenges in the Art and Science of Nursing." *The Lancet* 351 (1998): 438-440.

[18] House of Lords, *Report of the Select Committee of the House of Lords on Metropolitan Hospitals with Minutes of Evidence, Appendix and Index,*Vol. XVI. London: HMSO [Irish University Press Series of British Parliamentary Papers, vol. 12. Eds. Ford, P. and Ford, G. Shannon: Irish University, 1890. 167 para. 2567].

[19] House of Lords 1890, 167 para. 2534.

"Carry that bedpan to the glory of God."[20] But what made these privileged women take on such physically demanding, dangerous, low-status and low-paying work?

3. Evidence for the traditional nursing ethic

From whatever class the woman originated she was taught to be willing to turn her hand to any work that she saw needed doing. A nursing writer in 1893 said that: "work, that some people term 'menial,' is not menial when done by her with that 'tincture' which George Herbert says, makes even 'drudgery divine.'"[21] The purpose of nursing was not occupational status, or the fulfillment of the individual nurse, it was the good of the patient.

Because the end or purpose of nursing was clear, the aim of the apprenticeship training was to produce practitioners fit for the purpose. The goal was to produce nurses not only with certain skills, but most importantly, who had the right qualities and attributes: a good "character." Nightingale constantly used this word to her probationers, and she had herself developed this approach from a Lutheran foundation. In Nightingale's view: "A woman cannot be a good and intelligent nurse without being a good and intelligent woman."[22] Nursing training was ultimately a moral educative process into which student nurses were inducted.

According to Nightingale, the nurse's primary responsibility was to the patient, the epicenter of her thinking:

> The nurse must have simplicity and a single eye to the patient's good. She must make no demand upon the patient for reciprocation, for acknowledgement or even perception of her services; since the best service a nurse can give *is* that the patient shall scarcely be aware of any and shall perceive her presence only by perceiving that he has *no* wants. The nurse must always be kind, but never emotional. The patient must find a real, not forced or "put on," centre of calmness in his nurse.[23]

Nightingale, a passionate statistician, was intensely practical. The nurse's character was manifested through the tasks and procedures of care and the diligence and precision they involved. This was the *carefulness* of care. Nightingale described such procedures in minute detail. Seeming unimportant and insignificant matters such as how urinals should be washed out, how chamber utensils should always be kept covered when not in use and when carried, and that urinals should never be left under the bed but beside the patient and emptied immediately after use were the vital details that differ-

[20] "The Bedpan Round." [editorial] *Nursing Times* March 8 1963: 281.
[21] Dannatt, A. *How to Become a Hospital Nurse.* London: Record, 1893. 30.
[22] Nightingale, F. "Nurses, Training of," and "Nursing the Sick." *A Dictionary of Medicine* [part II]. Ed. Quain R. London: Longmans, Green, and Co. 1882. 1038-1049.
[23] Nightingale 1882, 1049.

entiated good care from bad care. Hygiene of the nurse's skin, including short nails, and careful washing and scrubbing of surgical instruments and dressing forceps were vital to prevent infection.

Precision, gentleness, and infinite carefulness was the basis for her nurse training school founded at St Thomas's Hospital in London. It was for every ward sister to *show* every new probationer how to do her work, not only how it should be done, but also to guard against how it should not be done. An adequate medical knowledge in subjects such as chemistry, anatomy, and physiology was to be learned from a medical instructor and examined both orally and in writing, in order that the nurse's powers of expression to train others would thereby be developed. A good library was important. Careful jottings of doctors' comments and notes of cases were to be recorded, so that the nurse learned to observe and understand her own cases and "learn the reason of what is done" so that she would be enabled to teach others.

Although the nurse was expected to obey the physician's or surgeon's directions, this was an intelligent obedience using discretion realizing these were conditional.[24] The key to authority, in having control over others, according to Nightingale, was to have control over oneself by "the silent power of a consistent life." Here there could be no pretence or dissimulation. In exercising authority nurses should not "try to 'seem' anything, but to *be* what we would *seem*."[25]

Nursing textbooks for a century reflected this Nightingale ideal. Matrons, tutors, and ward sisters constantly reiterated the same message, even as their books changed through editions to recognize scientific advances: the ethical basis of nursing arises from the moral character of the nurse and the moral ethos in which she, and later also he, was trained and worked. This was the framework on which rested technical knowledge and skills, powers of observation, attention to the intimate practical details of personal hygiene and comfort. Order, structure, diligence, supervision, and method were crucial. Character formed the kindness of the nurse's manner and approach towards the patient.

The inexperienced nurse was inducted gradually into care in which the wisdom and sensitivity needed to touch the human body was learned. The good nurse did not regard some tasks as menial and unworthy to be handed down to others who were less elevated. Washing the patient, as well as deal-

---

[24] Nightingale, F. *Florence Nightingale to Her Nurses.* Ed. Nash, R. London: Macmillan, 1914. 11.

[25] Nightingale 1914, 12-13.

ing with excrement, urine, vomit, sputum, and his soiled body, were an essential part of care. Nurses in this Nightingale tradition were not dealing with the technical or spiritual or emotional separately, as if this was a higher plane; they were dealing with the *person* in his or her wholeness, including the technical and spiritual and emotional, but also, and crucially, the physical base–the diseased and often broken body. To become a nurse was not just to enter into a contractual obligation dependent on reward; it was to enter into a covenant that existed regardless of reciprocation.

4. The wider moral context of nursing

What is described above is a tradition of nursing care in which the good nurse was the virtuous nurse, and as one nursing writer, Derek Sellman, eloquently shows, this approach to nursing ethics has become sadly neglected in modern nurse education.[26] In that context, Sellman, drawing on Alasdair MacIntyre's *After Virtue*,[27] proposes an examination of these virtues from an Aristotelian perspective. But certainly an analysis of virtues and their crucial importance to nursing needs to go beyond Aristotle, to the primary virtue necessary to motivate people to care for the weak and seemingly unattractive in a self-sacrificial way. For this virtue, as MacIntyre himself argues, comes from a tradition other than that of Aristotle and ancient Greece; it derives from the Judeo-Christian tradition which no doubt built on Aristotle's worldview, but also went beyond it.

MacIntyre acknowledges that the concept of charity, of which Aristotle knew nothing, is not merely one more virtue to be added to the list of relevant virtues; it alters the conception of the good for human beings in a radical way. "Care" as love or charity is the prime moral commandment of the Judeo-Christian tradition, profoundly differentiating it from previous moral traditions. So for example, Aristotle's account of human nature expressed in the virtues has no place for humility or charity, which were considered to be fundamental virtues for the good nurse. Love then, is not one virtue to be added to the others, but the basis of all the virtues. Those characteristics which are needed for the good (and for our purposes the good nurse) are not mere lists but coherent characteristics that derive from the common source of love or charity or *agape*.

MacIntyre's hypothesis is that the modern language of morality is in a state of grave disorder. We possess simulacra of morality; we continue to use many of the key expressions, but we have lost our comprehension, both

---

[26] Sellman, D. "The Virtues in the Moral Education of Nurses: Florence Nightingale revisited." *Nursing Ethics* 4.4 (1997): 3-11.

[27] MacIntyre, A. *After Virtue: A study in moral theory.* London: Duckworth, 1985².

theoretical and practical, of morality. While MacIntyre's argument is a criticism of post-Enlightenment society, his analysis readily translates to nursing and reveals the causes of the neglected tradition of virtue that Sellman mourns.

Nursing appears to be an almost perfect example of MacIntyre's analysis, whereby segments of modern culture take out the values of the past in which the profession was traditionally embedded and which defined the purpose of nursing practice, and instead seek to knit the fragmented and redefined values together in a new system and on a new basis. But it is difficult to find, in new theories of care constructed by philosophers,[28] moral reasons to submit oneself to the service of people who are strangers, and who may seem at times unattractive, unappreciative, difficult, and even dangerous. This is particularly the case given the kind of self-denying and compassionate service of washing, cleaning, and holding that being a nurse involves.

The problem is that divorced from its vocational tradition, we are without a common, intelligible language about nursing and its values of care. The result is evident in the current crisis and confusion about the nature, identity, and purpose of the nursing profession, as the tradition of what Gillon has called "simple service" is *de facto* if not *de iure* being abandoned. The universalizable moral principles which have underpinned the purpose of nursing as "simple service" have weakened, and to use Gillon's words, patients have become "shuttlecocks" in an interprofessional battle about the occupational status of nursing.

MacIntyre's analysis sheds light on the causes of this nursing rivalry. He writes that the whole notion of virtues, such as promise-keeping, truth-telling, and benevolence, is embodied in universalizable moral principles. The traditional concept of the authority of such moral principles derives not from attitudes, preferences, or feelings, but from the embodied ethical tradition of a community's moral order. Removed from this concrete tradition such values become merely arbitrary and subjective, nothing more than choices of individuals engaged in incommensurable rival arguments. There are no objective criteria to choose between them.

This vacuum leads to three characteristics of contemporary ethical debate. Firstly, arguments based on rival premises possess no rational way of weighing the claims of one against the other. Each premise uses a different normative or evaluative concept from the others so that claims made on us

---

[28] Noddings, N. *Caring: A feminine approach to ethics and moral education.* Berkeley: University of California, 1984; Blustein, J. *Care and Commitment: Taking the personal point of view.* Oxford: Oxford University, 1991.

are of different kinds. Because rival arguments reach rival conclusions and cannot be assailed on the grounds of reason, they become the subject of assertion and counter-assertion. This is the second characteristic of contemporary debate. Shrillness enters, and there is a clash of wills, each determined by arbitrary choices of its own, which are in reality matters only of taste. This stalemate leads to masquerade: the pretence of an appeal to an objective and universalizable standard.

The third characteristic of contemporary debate, MacIntyre argues, is intimately connected to these first two. Conceptually incommensurable premises of rival arguments have a wide variety of historical origins. Moreover the concepts we employ have in some cases changed their character over centuries; the variety of expressions we use have changed their meaning. He writes, "In the transition from the variety of contexts in which they were originally at home to our own contemporary culture 'virtue' and 'justice' and 'piety' and 'duty' and even 'ought' have become other than they once were."[29]

And so today, the current misunderstanding and sidelining of nursing tradition, in which the vocation and its underlying premise is repudiated and even ridiculed, reveals that there is no longer a moral vocabulary to apply to nursing. It has lost its meaning for the present because we have only fragments of the conceptual scheme of nursing from the past. The contexts from which their significance derived is not understood because it is unknown. Meanwhile the language and appearance of nursing as "caring" and "compassion" persist even though their substance has been largely fragmented and destroyed (MacIntyre's masquerade). Rivalries ensue about the culture, status, and purpose of nursing, alienating nurses who want to practice plain and simple caring and perplexing commentators and patients who still assume the inherited nursing tradition exists.

For MacIntyre modern morality is doomed to fail unless it takes cognizance of the moral tradition in which it is embedded. MacIntyre claims that historically this moral tradition is an account of morality which derives from the virtues of the human character and which is inextricably tied to the purpose of human life. It is a living tradition which is historically extended and socially embodied. Within a living tradition the pursuit of goods extends through generations. The individual's search for his or her good is generally and characteristically conducted within a context that is defined by those traditions of which the individual life is part. Embedding is crucial.

This is the point of relevance to nursing. Historically, the individual nurse was embedded in a tradition of care greater than herself. Just as the human individual is inseparable from his or her role in society, so the nurse

---

[29] MacIntyre 1985, 10.

was inseparable from her role in meeting the needs of society's sick and preventing sickness itself. As the virtues are those traits of character that the individual needs to fulfill that role, so the nurse needed to be molded into the character of care. Individual actions and activities, which cannot be interpreted apart from their narrative history, itself embedded in the tradition, came alive for the nurse who existed because of the tradition of nursing into which she was inducted.

For MacIntyre there is a unity to life. The individual person lives out his or her life for the end or purpose that governs that life. Life cannot be separated into individual activities, the personal and private, or the public and professional, or indeed into separate ages, such as childhood and old age. Rather, life is unitary, it is conceived and evaluated as a whole in the light of the purpose and end to which it is destined, "the good." The virtues are those dispositions which enable us to fulfill this life and achieve "the good" and better understand the nature and character of "the good." From this perspective the purpose of the nurse is to fulfill this "good" for those in need of care. Nursing has no other purpose.

5. The lesson from history

The lesson from history, then, is the call for the nursing profession to renew its purpose. With a central focus on the needs of patients and clients, nursing will be able to redefine the nurse's professional responsibility. From nursing tradition we see that medical science had crucial effects for the prevention, eradication, and mitigation of illness and disease. As Nightingale knew, the nurse has a central role and purpose in such advances for the benefit of patients and society as a whole. And this advancement continues even more rapidly today. Education that prepares nurses to be competent in these aspects of both knowledge and skill is crucial, so that the nurse can fulfill this role effectively. This medical know-how is part of the purpose of nursing.

But it is only a part of the purpose. People still become vulnerable and need to be cared for as they become sick, and age, and eventually die. The pastoral and personal side of nursing, that was so important for Nightingale, remains crucial at the start of the twenty-first century. Nightingale taught that this central aspect of the nurse's role could not be learned in a classroom or from books because it was unspoken and unarticulated. The way to become a good nurse was to watch and learn how other good nurses built relationships with patients and carried out the practical tasks of caring for them. This internship was an induction into a living tradition of virtue, and it is no less vital today than it was in Nightingale's day.

Now, and in the future, nurses need to be inducted into the unchanging moral approach to care that is its tradition; so they need to develop the kind

33

of character which treats the patient with humanity, compassion, and gentleness, and values the human body in all its burden and weakness. For the patient, vulnerability brings with it the need for comfort and security. As Nightingale understood, care is needed which is precise, ordered, methodical, and supervised. Good nursing depends on this moral framework. It cannot so much be taught, but rather it is caught by watching other good nurses who have themselves learned to demonstrate virtuous care.

6. Conclusion

This chapter has argued that the central purpose of nursing is to be found in this inseparable combination of art and science, competence and compassion. Technical competence is necessary but not sufficient. The moral framework underpinning the nurse's care is vital to keep alive the central purpose of nursing: the readiness to attend to the smallest practical details of personal care, comforting, chatting with, holding hands with, stroking, feeding, grooming, washing, bathing, cleaning. The nurse's professional responsibility is built on an enduring and universal moral framework; it is not a self-conscious duty but a relationship to the person in need, a joyful and unspoken gift of the human spirit.

This chapter is further developed in Bradshaw, A. *The Nurse Apprentice, 1860-1977.* Aldershot: Ashgate, 2001; Bradshaw, A. *The Project 2000 Nurse: The remaking of British general nursing, 1978-2000.* London: Whurr, 2001.

Discussion questions

1. Read the vignette again. Describe the relationship between the registered nurse and the patient.

2. How does the student nurse, Paul, learn from Jane Smith?

3. What makes Jane Smith a good nurse?

4. How does Jane Smith cope with her own irritation at Mr. Brown's demands?

5. Explain what role nursing history might have in developing different answers to these questions?

4

Communicating Christian Conviction

Ethics of spiritual care

Arlene B. Miller

Vignette

Sarah was making a home visit to see a young mother with congestive heart failure. A relative from India had come to stay with her and care for her two young sons. The patient could no longer climb the stairs to her bedroom. She was on a waiting list for a heart transplant as her best hope for continued life. During the course of the visit the patient pointed out a picture of "my God." Sarah saw a faded photograph of what she assumed was a Hindu guru. Sarah, a Christian nurse, wondered how to meet the spiritual needs of this woman. What should she say or do?

1. Introduction

Many accept spiritual care today as part of nursing along with care of the body and mind. In this chapter we will explore the history of how this inclusion came about.

- Specifically, we will consider cultural trends that have shaped modern nursing and the way nurses think about spiritual care. We will also discuss the work of several Christian nurses who influenced the move to include spiritual care in nursing (section 2).
- We will also identify some ethical issues associated with spiritual care in nursing. In order to deal with these issues we will first develop a biblical understanding of spirit and the needs of the spirit (section 3).
- Having established the meaning of Christian spiritual care (supporting and fostering a patient's relationship with God), we then respond to the ethical concerns from a Christian perspective (section 4).
- In the final stage of our discussion, we address the professional nurse's stance in spiritual care.

Our conclusion is that Christian spiritual care fits within this book's "ethic of responsibility" because the well-being of patients, which nurses' professional responsibility seeks to foster, includes spiritual well-being.

2. Background

2.1 *Cultural and societal impact on nursing.*

Nursing's roots are deep in Christianity. Caring for the sick, even those outside the family, was considered a natural extension of Christ's ministry of healing. Deaconesses and religious orders were devoted to nursing. Florence Nightingale took her inspiration from these Christian orders. Her determination to make nursing a secular calling was intended to open its ranks to Christian women of all churches and to offer its services to all those who needed care irrespective of their faith. She did not intend that nursing become nonreligious even though many have taken this position to be her meaning.

However, Western societies became more pluralistic culturally and religiously. Nursing education moved into colleges and universities. Some nursing leaders perceived nursing's historical link with Christianity as an impediment to becoming a profession because it encouraged sacrifice, not the reforms they wanted. While some religious hospitals remained a large segment of health care, many nonreligious facilities were established. Many nurses were personally motivated by their Christian faith, but the nursing profession was and still is self-consciously secular.

Nursing students were taught such things as preparing patients for clergy visits and rituals of communion and baptism as well as dietary requirements of religious origin. The nurse's role was to support clergy and to respect the patient's practices. He or she was not expected to pray with patients or to read scripture or religious literature to them

2.2 Influences leading to spiritual care in nursing

We can ask, what has changed so that today nurses are again expected to give spiritual care? Barbara Stevens Barnum in *Spirituality in Nursing: From traditional to New Age* accounts for the concern for spiritual care in nursing by three recent trends.[1] First, the increasing number of substance abuse self-help programs stress reliance on a "higher power" for strength to overcome addictions. Second, she sees a "resurgence of attention to a spiritual dimension" among traditionally religious nurses. Finally, Barnum identifies the emergence of "New Age 'ideologies'" in larger society that are incorporated in more recent nursing theories.

Self-help programs were based on the Twelve-Step Program of Alcoholics Anonymous (AA). AA is based on Christian ideas of confession, forgiveness, trusting God for strength to overcome one's addiction, and relying on one's fellows for support and accountability. By using the term "higher power" for God, participants were left to their own understanding of God. We will see how this influence has been incorporated into nursing definitions of spirituality.

The traditionally religious nurses identified by Barnum were the ones motivated by their Christian faith to see nursing as a way to serve God and their fellow humans. Some of them managed to separate their faith and their nursing practice. Others, however, were never at ease with such separation and sought ways to bring their faith and work together.

The New Age ideologies in the larger society reflect a truth about humanity explained in Scripture. We are created to worship the One who created us. Even in rebellion against God, humans will continue to seek something beyond themselves to give meaning and purpose to life. Many in these New Age movements sought enlightenment through practices long associated with eastern religions such as Taoism, Hinduism, and Buddhism. Going beyond the rational process they reported experiences of being connected to all things, the breaking down of distinctions. Some nurse thinkers picked up these ideas in the term *holism*. New Age thinking often separated spirituality and religion. We will see how these ideas could be incorporated into nursing, even as a secular profession.

---

[1] Stevens Barnum, B. *Spirituality in Nursing: From traditional to New Age.* New York: Springer, 1996. 14.

2.3 Spiritual care in nursing literature

Nursing, as a cultural phenomenon, reflects current concepts and explanatory theories used in other disciplines. Accordingly, nurse theorists developed theories applying General Systems Theory, a philosophy of science propounded by biologist Ludwig von Bertalanffy.[2] For example, Betty Neuman first published her theory, The Neuman Systems Model, in 1972; four years after von Bertalanffy published his book. Imogene King's second book, *A Theory for Nursing: Systems, concepts, process* appeared in 1981. Systems theory provides a way for nurses to deal with complex interactions between persons and the many aspects of their environment, as well as interactions within the individual.

Neuman's and King's theories also incorporated the idea of *holism*.[3] For them the person is viewed as a whole and all dimensions–physical, psychological, and social–are attended to in care. The term originally did not carry the New Age connotations sometimes associated with it. Missing from these early nursing theories was a focus on spiritual care as such. Neuman later added a spiritual dimension in the second edition of her book.[4]

In 1978 a widely used medical-surgical nursing textbook, *Clinical Nursing: Pathophysiological and psychosocial approaches* by Irene L. Beland and Joyce Y. Passos,[5] included an epilog titled "Spiritual Dimensions of Nursing Practice." The authors of the epilog, Jean Stallwood and Ruth Stoll, were professors of nursing at government-funded universities in the United States. They presented a Conceptual Model of Man's Nature that placed spirit (God-consciousness, relatedness to deity) at the core of the person, surrounded by a psychosocial layer (soul, self-consciousness, self-identity) and an outer biological layer (five senses and world consciousness). The model represents a systems approach; in that interaction takes place among all aspects of the person. The model is *holistic* in that the person is viewed as a whole, even though distinctions are made among the differing "dimensions" of the person. The authors use *holism* in the sense of attending to all aspects of the person (physical, emotional, intellectual, etc.) and meeting spiritual needs as one aspect of nursing care.

---

[2] King, I.M. *A Theory for Nursing: Systems, concepts, process.* New York: John Wiley & Sons, 1981.

[3] We can distinguish between two meanings of *holism*. The first is a comprehensive approach to anything, considering all parts or dimensions of a person or object. The second is a philosophy that only looks at things without making distinctions between the whole and the parts. Nurse theorists often refer to South African statesman and philosopher, Jan (Christian) Smuts (1870-1950), as an early proponent of the philosophy of *holism*.

[4] Neuman, B. *The Neuman Systems Model* (2nd ed.). Norwalk: Appleton Lange.

[5] Beland, I.L. and Passos, J.Y. eds. *Clinical Nursing: Pathophysiological and psychological approaches.* New York: Macmillan, 1975, 1983.

Stallwood and Stoll define spiritual needs as "any factors necessary to establish and maintain a person's dynamic personal relationship with God (as defined by that individual)."[6] Here we see the influence of the self-help movement in referring to God in a generic way. They identify five spiritual needs common to all persons: forgiveness, love, hope, trust and meaning and purpose in life. They suggest nursing approaches to meet these needs including counseling (problem solving), prayer, and using scripture and other literature. For the first time in a major nursing text, nurses were told to include specific nursing interventions directed toward spiritual care.[7]

Three years after Stallwood and Stoll's chapter, Virginia Henderson and Gladys Nite included an extensive chapter called "Worship" in the 6th edition of *Principles and Practice of Nursing*.[8] Henderson introduced the topic with "the search for meaning in life." Interestingly, she quotes Stallwood and Stoll from the earlier Beland text. Much of the chapter describes the major living religions so that nurses could understand patients' religious beliefs. A shorter section is devoted to ways in which nurses and others could help to meet spiritual needs, including listening, providing and supporting spiritual advisors requested by patients, administering sacraments when necessary, and reading prayers and other literature requested by patients. Again nurses are expected to include meeting spiritual needs in patient care although most of the interventions are the more traditional support of clergy and respecting specific religious practices of patients such as diet and rituals. Henderson's theory of nursing is patient-focused and *holistic* in the sense of being comprehensive, considering all the needs of patients including the need to worship.

2.4 New Age theories in nursing

Since these earlier approaches to spiritual care, newer theories reflecting the emergence of "New Age 'ideologies'" in the larger culture, as noted above by Barnum, are being developed. Nurses can no longer assume that most of their patients will be associated with one of the major religions, which have usually been Christian or Jewish. Spirituality in newer nursing theories is generic and not associated with organized religion. The trend to

---

[6] Stallwood, J. and Stoll, R.I. "Spiritual Dimensions of Nursing Practice," in Beland and Passos 1975, 1087.

[7] In 1979, Ruth Stoll published an article in *American Journal of Nursing* 179.9 (Sept. 1979): 1574-77, titled, "Guidelines for Spiritual Assessment." She identified four categories of questions: concept of God or deity, sources of hope and strength, religious practices, and relationship between religion and health.

[8] Henderson, V. and Nite, G. *Principles and Practice of Nursing* (6th ed.). New York: Macmillan, 1978.

separate *spirituality* from religion is already present in the ideas of Stallwood and Stoll and Henderson, even though many interventions they suggest are associated with Christian and Jewish religions.

Barnum sees these "New Age" theories as the "fastest growing trend in nursing."[9] She identifies three representative theorists: Jean Watson, Margaret Newman, and Barbara Dossey and colleagues.[10] These theories are "spiritual" in the sense that they have some concept of humans in relation to spirit or God. But, in contrast to more traditional theories such as Neuman's or King's, the link is within the person himself or herself and not a relationship with a personal God. Persons are primarily spirits, and health is striving for transcendence and union with a nonpersonal consciousness or realizing one's own divinity.

According to these theories *holism* reflects the New Age understanding that all things are interconnected and that the larger environment is contained within the individual, even the smallest aspects of the person. Hence, analysis of the bio-psycho-social dimensions is not stressed in this type of theory. What is emphasized is the spiritual nature of the whole person. The nurse gives spiritual care by helping patients move along in their spiritual development. The most common interventions include "life-energy" therapies of various kinds, guided imagery and other mental therapies, and different forms of spiritism including channeling and shamanistic rituals. Prayer may or may not be addressed to a god separate and distinct from the one who prays. If it is directed to a "god," the individual defines that god. Often prayer is merely good intentions on the part of the nurse healer toward the ill person.

Further evidence that spiritual care is considered part of nursing is its inclusion in the taxonomies of nursing diagnosis and interventions developing in North America. The North American Nursing Diagnosis Association (NANDA) lists *spiritual distress* in its taxonomy.[11] The Nursing Interventions Classification (NIC) developed by the Iowa Intervention Project, a group of nurse educators and researchers at the University of Iowa, includes the intervention *Spiritual Support* with a list of suggested activities.[12]

---

[9] Stevens Barnum, B.J. *Nursing Theory: Analysis, application, evaluation* (4th ed.). Philadelphia: Lippincott, 1994, 99.

[10] Stevens Barnum 1996, 75.

[11] Carpenito, L.J. *Nursing Diagnosis: Application and clinical practice* (7th ed.). Philadelphia: Lippincott, 1997. 872.

[12] McCloskey, J.C. and Bulecheck, G.M. eds. *Nursing Interventions* (2nd ed.), St. Louis: Mosby, 1996. 517.

We have traced the way in which spiritual care has come to be included in nursing theory and in nursing education. In many nursing schools students are introduced to spiritual care as part of nursing. Sometimes they are taught the traditional ways such as knowing when to call the chaplain or priest and providing privacy for the visit. Others are taught New Age practices such as Therapeutic Touch and shamanism. Graduate programs allow more time for these various approaches.

2.5 Impact of Christian nurses on spiritual care in nursing

We now turn to the work of Barnum's "traditionally religious nurses" and their work in developing spiritual care as part of nursing. In fact, it was Christian nurses on the National Group for the Classification of Nursing Diagnosis (precursor of NANDA) who introduced the diagnosis, *alterations in faith*, later changed to the current, *spiritual distress*. So, it was the "traditional Christian" nurses who opened this door in the early 1970s. The textbooks published by major publishing companies and educational theories we discussed above followed.

The *Journal of Christian Nursing*, first published in 1984, became the voice for nurse writers who wanted to write from the perspective of their Christian faith. This journal, listed in the Cumulative Index of Nursing and Allied Health Literature (CINAHL) carries accounts of how nurses give spiritual care. It published many of the first articles on spiritual care in nursing.

Judith Allen Shelly and Sharon Fish wrote the first edition of *Spiritual Care: The nurse's role* in 1978, revising it twice since.[13] Rather than turning to major publishers, these authors choose to stay with Christian publishing companies to retain a distinctly Christian approach. Shelly recently authored *Spiritual Care: A guide for caregivers*, written more broadly for anyone in a caring role.[14] Nurses Christian Fellowship, USA, created a task force that in 1990 published *Concepts in Nursing: A Christian perspective*, edited by Ruth I. Stoll.[15] Sr. Mary Elizabeth O'Brien wrote *Spirituality in Nursing: Standing on holy ground* in 1999 and *The Nurse's Calling: A Christian spirituality of caring for the sick* in 2001.[16] All of these publications assume that spiritual care is indeed part of nursing and that it should be Christian in nature. Nurses are

---

[13] Fish, S. and Shelly, J.A. *Spiritual Care: The nurse's role*. Downers Grove: InterVarsity, 1978.

[14] Shelly, J.A. *Spiritual Care: A guide for caregivers*. Downers Grove: InterVarsity, 2000.

[15] Stoll, R.I. ed. *Concepts in Nursing: A Christian perspective*. Madison: Nurses Christian Fellowship of InterVarsity Christian Fellowship, 1990.

[16] O'Brien, M.E. *Spirituality in Nursing: Standing on holy ground*. Boston: Jones and Bartlett, 1999; *The Nurse's Calling: A Christian spirituality of caring for the sick*. New York: Paulist, 2001.

urged to speak openly of their faith, to pray and read scripture with patients as well as provide compassionate nursing care.

Ann Bradshaw, also writing from a Christian perspective, takes a somewhat different approach in her 1994 *Lighting the Lamp: The spiritual dimension of nursing care.*[17] She stresses Christian theology as the basis for defining the person and the motivation for giving care. She decries the substitution of professionalism for Christian love, *agape,* in nursing as undermining the spiritual nature of caring for the bodily needs of patients. For Bradshaw, nursing as it has been traditionally understood is spiritual by nature. However, she does not assign to nurses such interventions as prayer and Bible-reading. Relying on a team approach she leaves these to clergy who are the specialists and those from whom patients expect such care.

3. Ethical issues associated with spiritual care in nursing
3.1 Locating the issues

Thus far we have considered how spiritual care has come to be regarded as part of the nurse's role, at least in the view of theorists and educators. However, it is one thing to teach nursing students that they should meet spiritual needs of their patients. It is another thing for them to actually do so in the clinical setting or to implement policies on spirituality in modern health care settings. Attempting to do so raises many questions and ethical issues.

One set of questions concerns how nurses can assess the spiritual needs of their patients. For example, can they be assessed the same way that physical pain is assessed on a continuum of 1 to 10? Can treatment interventions be expected to lead to defined outcomes in the same way that calibrating a dosage of insulin to achieve a certain blood glucose level should do?

A second set of questions related to the first set revolves around the understanding of spiritual needs. How do spiritual needs differ from psychological and social needs? There is no single accepted understanding in the literature. René van Leeuwen, nurse educator in the Netherlands, conducted research using a panel of expert nurses regarding the relevance of a patient's spirituality for nursing. The panel did agree that it was relevant but could not reach consensus regarding the definition of *spiritual distress* as a nursing diagnosis.[18] The answer to this question depends to a great extent on

---

[17] Bradshaw, A. *Lighting the Lamp: The spiritual dimension of nursing care.* Oxford: Scutari, 1994.
[18] Leeuwen, R.R. van, and Hunink, G.H. "Spiritual Distress," *Verpleegkunde* 15.1 (2000): 41-49 [in Dutch].

whether spirituality is viewed from a generic perspective or from a religious context.

A third group of questions concerns what patients expect of nurses who care for them. Do they think they have been given poor care if they have not been asked about their spiritual beliefs and offered specific interventions? Do they welcome this type of care or are they offended when it is offered?

A fourth cluster of questions focuses on what employing agencies want from nurses. What do these employers expect of the nurses they hire? Most health care facilities have prohibitions against proselytizing by employees because they reflect our culturally and religiously pluralistic societies. Is assessing a patient's spiritual needs an integral part of the nursing assessment? Are nurses expected to meet those needs or should clergy or other religious specialists be called upon? Should nurses who serve in a society which forbids sharing one's faith break the law of the land and risk their own personal safety?

A fifth group of questions concerns nurses who give spiritual care. Is assessing and meeting spiritual needs a nursing skill that can be taught? Can all nurses be equally expected to provide spiritual care interventions? Barnum asks whether a certain level of spiritual maturity of the nurse is essential to qualify for giving spiritual care. Is spiritual care a nursing specialty? What if the nurse's religious beliefs differ from those of the patient? Whose beliefs take priority–those of the patient or of the nurse? Are nurses expected to participate in rituals based on beliefs different or opposed to their own beliefs? Barnum wonders if meeting the spiritual needs of patients might become the primary motive for nursing. Should it?

3.2 How do we learn truth about the spirit?

We will begin by considering the first and second sets of foundational questions: 1) How do nurses assess the spiritual needs of their patients, and 2) What are the spiritual needs of their patients, the needs of their spirits? How we respond to the other ethical issues identified above very much depends on how we answer these two. We find a number of perspectives or worldviews in the nursing literature concerning spirit and spiritual needs. Thus, we ask a further question. Is there a truthful way to talk about spiritual needs or is the answer merely a matter of personal perception? Truth here means *thinking and talking about things the way they really are*. If there is truth about spiritual needs, where and how do we get knowledge of it?

We get information concerning the functioning of patients' bodies by a multitude of assessment techniques from simple ones like touching or tak-

43

ing a temperature to complex ones like heart catheterizations and magnetic resonance imaging (MRI). Further, we interpret the findings from these techniques in the context of what has been learned about the body through years of scientific study. The body we can see, feel, hear, measure, and weigh. But the spirit? The spirit is not accessible to such techniques. How then do we learn about the needs of the spirit?

We need to push back even further by asking what is *spirit?* One dictionary definition is that spirit is "that which constitutes one's unseen, intangible being; the essential and activating principle of a person; the will."[19] This definition is helpful in that it tells us that people are more than what can be seen and measured. It also explains why we are unable to learn about the spirit through the usual clinical assessment tools. However, the definition is unhelpful in that it is abstract and leaves us wondering about the nature of this intangible aspect of being.[20] If nurses are to give ethical spiritual care they need to know more.

3.3 A biblical understanding of spirit

For this further understanding, Christians turn to Scripture, the written record of truth God has revealed about himself and his Creation.[21] In the Creation narrative we are told that humans have qualities and abilities that mirror those of God, the Creator.

> Then God said, "Let us make humankind in our image, according to our likeness; and let them have dominion over the fish of the sea, and over the birds of the air, and over the cattle, and over all the wild animals of the earth, and over every creeping thing that creeps upon the earth." So God created humankind in his image, in the image of God he created them; male and female he created them (Genesis 1:26-27, NRSV).[22]

These God-like qualities enable us to act for God in the created world, to be his agents in bringing the earth to fruition. In carrying out this awesome responsibility we are given authority for which we are accountable to God.

We learn further that God created people as social beings, male and female, to love and share life with one another and with the Creator God himself (Genesis 2:18-25). In these relationships they reflect the love and

---

[19] *The American Heritage Dictionary of the English Language.* New College Edition, Boston: Houghton Mifflin, 1975.
[20] This definition also reduces the human spirit to will. Some would include will as one aspect of the spirit but certainly not the only aspect.
[21] I assume the trustworthiness and authority of Scripture in this chapter.
[22] New Revised Standard Version of the Bible (NRSV). In this chapter all quotations from the Bible are in this version.

communication that characterizes the relationship of the Father, the Son, and the Spirit, the triune God.[23]

We are also told that God breathed his very own life into the beings he formed from the *tangible dust of the ground*: "then the LORD God formed man from the dust of the ground, and breathed into his nostrils the breath of life; and the man became a living being" (Genesis 2:7). No other created being received God's life in this way. Animals, birds, and fish were "spoken" into existence. People–nurses, patients, families, and co-workers–reflect God's personal nature in this God-breathed life, this intangible aspect of their being within God-formed bodies.

We can think, then, of persons both as embodied spirits and inspirited bodies. People are personal beings just as God is personal although we are in a limited creaturely way. People are spiritual beings just as God is spiritual although the human spirit is dependent on God's Spirit for its life (Genesis 3:8-10). People are personal beings as God is personal because they are spiritual beings like God.[24]

Jesus reinforces this understanding when he tells a woman with whom he was having a religious discussion that God is spirit, and that those who worship him must worship in spirit and in truth (John 4:23-24). John, the apostle, tells us that no one has ever seen God (John 1:18).

What, then, is spirit? *The human spirit is the God-breathed, God-imaging personal life.* The spirit is that which makes humans personal beings, in contrast to other living creatures. In other words, *the personal aspect of a person is the spiritual aspect of that person.* This definition has vast implications for what we mean by spiritual care. Before turning to these implications, however, we need to consider how God sustains the life he breathed into humans.

One way of sustaining our spirits is through fellowship with other people. People are fundamentally social beings. God provided for this need by creating two persons from one, two different and complementary people, a man and a woman. They were to be companions in the responsibilities

---

[23] Genesis 2:18-25. The Trinitarian nature of God (Father, Son, and Spirit) is the basis for the social nature of persons. We see the first hints of this in Genesis 1:26: "Then God said, 'Let us make humankind in our image.'" In the New Testament the "three persons/One God" nature of God was more fully disclosed in Jesus, as he spoke of God as his Father, as the Spirit of God, and himself as the Son of God. At Jesus' baptism by his cousin John all three persons are identified as being present. See Matthew 3:16-17. Later the church fathers formalized this doctrine of the Trinity in the several creeds.

[24] We refer to people as *spiritual beings* in this chapter. God also is a spiritual being. There are other spiritual beings, i.e. angels, both good and evil. While angels may take on bodily appearance according to Scripture there is no record of their being formed of the "dust of the earth." (Genesis 2:7). Humans are unique in that they are both spiritual and earthly.

given them by God. Because they were spiritual, they could encourage and sustain each other's spirits (Genesis 2:18-25).

Yet human fellowship alone is not sufficient; we need fellowship with the source of spiritual life, God the Creator. We are told that God himself came to our first parents in the garden of their home. In Genesis 3:8 we are given a glimpse of the fellowship of God and our first parents by which he sustained their spirits.

With these truths in mind we can talk about spirit on two levels,
- the horizontal or human, and
- the vertical or divine.

This understanding helps to clarify how nursing interventions for meeting psychosocial needs and spiritual needs often look alike. Barnum notes this issue when she comments that much of what is called spiritual care is really humanistic care.[25]

3.4 Psychosocial or spiritual care?

In the chapter "Compassionate Presence" in Shelly's *Spiritual Care* written for Christian caregivers, some of the interventions she discusses could just as well be characterized as psychosocial or humanistic nursing care. She includes active listening, empathy, vulnerability, humility, and commitment as practices that can be learned through faith, education, and practice.[26] In a later chapter she advocates the use of appropriate touch.[27] Every one of these practices is discussed in nursing texts concerning patient relationships or psychiatric nursing.[28] New Age spiritualities advocate all of these as well. One could ask, as Barnum does, what is spiritual about these practices?

The Creation narrative gives us a clue. Every person is a spiritual being, so it is fair to characterize personal relationships as spiritual relationships even though we usually call them psychosocial or interpersonal. Thus, when nurses relate to their patients endeavoring to understand and meet psychological and emotional needs, we can say they are meeting spiritual needs. Intentional listening and empathizing are ways of entering into a patient's personal or spiritual world. With education and practice nurses become skilled in such ways of caring. In much of the nursing literature concerning

---

[25] "Even when nurses give religious advice, it may be difficult to segregate their prescriptions from those holding simple humanistic values. This is particularly true for those elements expressed in the absence of verbal discussion of religion; for example soothing touch, presencing, and many forms of relieving suffering." Stevens Barnum 1994, 142.

[26] Shelly 2000, 75.

[27] Shelly 2000, 118.

[28] Many of the (NIC) interventions for *spiritual support* are similar to those listed under *emotional support* and *anxiety reduction*. McCloskey and Bulechek 1996. 109, 249, 517.

spiritual care, these interpersonal communication practices are what is meant by spiritual care. There is no link to religion, and there is general agreement that nurses should do these things. Health care facilities have no policies forbidding them. Even though the nurse and the patient have differing spiritual practices and religious beliefs, they can agree that nurses should listen carefully and be empathetic in their responses.

3.5 The broken spiritual relationship with God[29]

The second way to view spirit and spiritual care is the vertical or the divine aspect. We saw in the Creation narrative how a personal Creator God created people who mirrored his qualities and abilities, albeit in a much smaller and creaturely way. God created us to respond to him, carry out his mandates, act for him in Creation, and to love and communicate with him.

However, the first humans chose to overreach the power and authority given them by God, leading to cosmic disruptions in Creation (Genesis 3). Now, instead of welcoming God when he came to them, they hid from him in fear. Fearful of God, people began fearing and hating each other. We learn of the first sibling rivalry and murder (Genesis 5). The broken personal spiritual relationship between people and God led to broken personal spiritual relationships between persons. Now, each person's spirit is separated from the ultimate source of life, God's life. While we are still spiritual beings, we are now spiritually "dead" beings because we are alienated from God, the source of our life.

God warned that disobeying him would bring death, the fulfillment of which we see in ourselves and in those for whom we care (Genesis 2:15-17). We see the inevitable physical death we all must face. We see spiritual death in broken human relationships, in lonely patients. We see soul-destroying guilt weighing on many patients. We see the deep fear of death that saps hope and joy (Hebrews 2:15). The fractured relationship between the Creator and his human creatures is the *ultimate* source of these problems. No longer in relationship with its Creator, the human spirit is dead, and this death is manifested by fear, guilt, hopelessness, and damaged social relationships.

---

[29] In a technical sense everyone has a relationship with God whether or not they know it. In this chapter I am using the term "relationship with God" in the sense of a restored relationship in which a person can come to God with confidence because of Jesus Christ and his redemptive work.

3.6 Reestablishing the spiritual relationship with God

Now we can begin to identify spiritual needs. They are often defined in nursing literature as the need for love and relatedness, the need for forgiveness, the need for meaning and purpose in life, and the need for hope. There are probably other ways to categorize the needs of the spirit, but these four are a good beginning. Many of these can be met on a human level, at least temporarily. But ultimately we only find them fully met in a living relationship with God where his life once again sustains our spirits.

We are led to conclude that *ultimate* spiritual care involves supporting and facilitating a patient's relationship with God.[30] The goal of spiritual care is more than bringing comfort or better coping skills, although a healed relationship with God may indeed bring both. This essential spiritual relationship can then lead to the restoration of other personal relationships and the meeting of other spiritual needs. Christians know that God, in Jesus Christ, provides the way to restore spiritual life. It is Jesus, then, who ultimately can meet the needs of the spirit.

No longer are we talking about humanistic care alone, or a generic spirituality apart from religion. We are talking about the remedy for the deepest human problems, Jesus Christ "the Way, the Truth, and the Life" (John 14:6). We are talking about *spiritual truth*. Sharing the Good News is Christian spiritual care.

4. A Christian response to ethical issues of spiritual care

Herein lays the ethical dilemma for Christian nurses. In religiously pluralistic societies it is assumed that spiritual truth is individualistic and private. Religion should be kept out of public life and, like politics, is a topic to be avoided to keep peace. This privatization of faith is the world in which Christian nurses work. Policies in secular health care facilities usually forbid personnel to initiate discussions of religion with patients. Even more they proscribe proselytizing (attempting to convert patients to the spiritual beliefs or religion of their caregivers). We now turn to the ethical issues identified earlier in this chapter.

4.1 What do employers expect?

What are the ethics of providing spiritual care in this ultimate sense for Christian nurses in pluralistic societies? We begin with what employing agencies want from the nurses they hire. Most of them expect spiritual care

---

[30] Shelly, J.A. and Miller, A.B. *Called to Care: A Christian theology of nursing.* Downers Grove: InterVarsity, 1999. 229.

to be given by the specialists, the clergy or the patient's own pastor or spiritual leader. Pastoral care or spiritual care departments exist for this purpose. Further, administrators do not look favorably on complaints that nurses and caregivers are "pushing religion on patients."

Patients and employees represent a spectrum of faiths and spiritual practices. Anyone who claims that her or his faith is true for everyone is viewed as being intolerant. The acceptable way to state one's faith is to couch it in terms of "this is truth for me." Christian nurses who believe that Jesus Christ is the only way to God should appreciate the prohibition against proselytizing. A nurse who practices Wicca, for example, is not free to press her beliefs on patients either.

What most employing agencies do expect of nurses is competence in assessment skills and care with the focus on physical and psychosocial needs. Management and organizational skills are also essential for the care of many critically ill patients. Rarely do employment interviews focus on the ability of nurses to give spiritual care as such. Most employers assume that nurses refer patients to chaplains when appropriate.

4.2 What do patients expect?

Next we turn to the expectations of patients. Do they expect to receive spiritual care from nurses? Some research shows that patients welcome questions about their spiritual well-being by physicians. Nursing research is generally concerned with how patients respond to nurse-initiated spiritual care. Anecdotal reports, however, indicate that some patients do request that nurses pray or read scripture for them,[31] and some research too indicates patients' openness to have health professionals initiate prayer or talk of finding peace with God.[32]

Patients are accustomed to assessment interviews and do not object to standard questions about their religion such as whether clergy should be contacted. They do not object to being asked about religious practices that require special diets or space and time for rituals. In the context of nursing assessment, most patients respond favorably to inquiries about what they believe about God or a higher power.

---

[31] Judy Shelly relates how a fearful woman insisted that she (Judy) pray for her after finishing her morning care. There are many other such stories told by nurses. Shelly and Miller 1999, 236.

[32] Steinhauser, K.A. et al. "Factors Considered Important at the End of Life by Patients, Family, Physicians, and Other Care Providers." *Journal of the American Medical Association* 284.19 (2000): 2476-2482 ; Soderstrom, K. and Martinson, I. "Patients' Spiritual Coping Strategies: A study of nurse and patient perspectives." *Oncology Nursing Forum* 14.2 (1987): 41-46.

Patients do want to be heard and have their concerns taken seriously. They appreciate the sensitive nurse who hears their fear, even though barely expressed. They welcome the comforting touch that expresses empathy and presence. They are relieved when nurses help them express a wish they have no words to say. In this sense patients expect spiritual care.

However, many, if not most patients would be surprised or offended if nurses began their care on each shift with a formal prayer or reading from a religious text. If asked, some might appreciate this practice as something over and above expected nursing care.[33] Early Christian hospitals held morning ward prayers before the day's work began. Some still recite prayers or rosaries over the intercommunication system. But such practices are increasingly rare in pluralistic societies. To go beyond formal standardized practices to inquire about a patient's relationship with God or to suggest that he or she ought to know God would be considered intrusive by many. It would be perceived as proselytizing.

We ask, "What is proselytizing?" A dictionary definition of *to proselytize* is to convert someone from one belief or faith to another. In most cultures this has a negative connotation. Does giving Christian spiritual care necessarily mean that we want to convert our patients? It may! Coming to God through Jesus would be the means of spiritual healing for many of our patients. However, merely bringing patients to our way of thinking is not our goal. Spiritual life is what we want for them. God alone gives spiritual life. The amazing thing is he sometimes chooses to use us in the process. Hence, we will suggest some answers to these questions towards the end of this chapter.

5. Spiritual care and professional nursing
5.1 Spiritual care giving: skill or character?

We now turn to questions concerning the nurse who God uses in giving spiritual care. Preparation for giving Christian spiritual care begins with the nurse. Acknowledging the presence of the Lord in our workplace, even secular places hostile to Christians, affirms the teaching of scripture that God is everywhere. We expect God to be working even when we are unaware. Offering our work and ourselves to him and petitioning his wisdom and strength at the beginning of a shift gives us confidence that he will work through us by his Spirit, often in ways we do not see. We *listen* for the Spirit to alert us to those patients with open hearts. Then we go about our work.

---

[33] Arline Zimmerman, R.N., Ph.D., now retired, tells how as a nursing student at a Christian college students would ask patients if they could pray before starting their care.

Bradshaw's understanding that nursing itself should be motivated by *agape* love is the next step. She sees all of nursing as spiritual including providing the best physical care given with love and skill. Such care may lead patients to question our motivation for what are often unpleasant tasks. Here is opportunity to simply state our Christian motivation. Our explanation should be simple and not a long sermon.[34]

Next, using our observation and communication skills, those taught in every nursing program, usually gives us clues to the kind of relationship our patients have with their Creator: trusting, unsure, confused, rebellious, guilt ridden, hate filled. What we learn this way goes far beyond the answers given in a formal assessment. Often we discover what practices are helpful for supporting or restoring their faith in God.

Here is where Barnum's question about which nurses are prepared to give spiritual care is important. She wants to know if this is a skill that can be taught. Does it depend upon the spiritual maturity of the nurse?[35]

The answer to both questions is "Yes." Observing and communicating are skills for which the fundamentals can be taught but which are developed and refined with experience. Patricia Benner's understanding of skill acquisition, from novice to expert, applies here.[36] The spiritual maturity of the nurse and his or her ability to give spiritual care is related to developing expertise in observing and communicating.

But Christian spiritual maturity goes further. Nurses who have a growing, deepening relationship with Jesus Christ are better prepared so that God can then touch others through them. Are we reading scripture with the intent of hearing him? Is our character being formed through obedience to him? Are we sensitive to the work of God's Spirit in our lives? Are we being healed of our own brokenness? Are we accountable to other mature Christians with whom we share our struggles? All of these help us to see clues of God's working in the hearts of our patients.

To answer Barnum's question, then, we can say that the basics of spiritual care can be taught, at least those psychosocial skills that meet spiritual needs on the human level. But the nurse who knows God's presence in his or her own life can become God's instrument for spiritual care in ways that go beyond these. Even more, those very psychosocial and communication skills are transformed to give true spiritual care.

---

[34] The Mennonite Central Committee (MCC), a relief and service agency, stamps the phrase, "In the name of Christ" on containers of food and supplies.

[35] Stevens Barnum 1996, 143.

[36] Benner, P. *From Novice to Expert: Excellence and power in clinical practice.* Menlo Park: Addison-Wesley, 1989.

An example of spiritual care

Phyllis Karns, Dean of the School of Nursing at Baylor University, wrote of her experience in spiritual care with two patients. A Jewish woman asked her how she handled stress in her life. Phyllis explained that Jesus Christ was the anchor who kept her steady in difficult times. Because the woman seemed interested, she went on to explain that Jesus was a Jew and that really Christianity grew out of the Old Testament. The woman acknowledged that she had some Jewish relatives who also worshipped Jesus as Messiah. Another one of Phyllis' patients was a young mother who was dying. Her biggest concern was leaving her children behind. Phyllis told her the bible story of Hannah who left her child in the care of Eli and trusted that God would look after him. Another story was of Jocobed, Moses' mother, who placed him in the little ark on the water trusting that God would provide for his care.[37]

The form spiritual care takes will differ with each person. It will be different for a Christian and a nonchristian. However, some general rules do apply. Spiritual care should never overwhelm a person who is particularly vulnerable because of illness. It should not be antagonistic or insulting. It is not an opportunity to "get on a soapbox" with your personal views. Instead, spiritual care is allowing the Holy Spirit to touch another person through you. That connection may take place through praying for a client or family–aloud, if appropriate, or silently. This prayer is not only for healing, comfort, or peace, but also for the Lord to make himself known in a special way through current circumstances. Spiritual care may also take place through discussing how God might be working in the patient's situation. It may be reading from the Bible or from other literature.[38]

5.2 Difference in religion between nurse and patient

We need to address the concern Barnum raised about the differences between the beliefs and religion of nurses and their patients.[39] Can, for example, a Christian nurse meet the expressed spiritual needs of a Hindu patient? On the humanistic level it may be possible to some extent. What if the patient wants the Christian nurse to read prayers to Krishna? This is more problematic. It depends on what "reading" means to the patient and to the nurse. It may be that in doing so we can get a glimpse into our patients' thinking that will show us how to pray for them. On the other hand we take seriously the Psalmist's concerns regarding those who worship other gods: "I will not take part in their sacrifices or even speak the name of their gods" (Psalm 16:4).

A Christian East-Indian nurse friend says that she would not pray to Krishna but would offer to pray to her own God. Usually her offer is ac-

---

[37] Karns, P.S. "Building a Foundation for Spiritual Care." *Journal of Christian Nursing* 8.3 (1991): 10-13.

[38] Karns 1991, 12-13.

[39] Stevens Barnum 1996, 140.

cepted. When asked if she would call a Hindu priest if requested by a patient, she said "Yes." Her response respects the freedom and noncoercion with which God offers his love to us.

5.3 Motivation for nursing

Should giving spiritual care become the primary motivation for Christian nurses? Are other nursing skills only means for attending to patients' spiritual needs and thus less important?

The example of Jesus gives us an answer to this question. His reason for coming to earth was to show us what God is like and to restore broken human relationships with him through his death and resurrection. He reconciled by meeting people where they were and tending to the needs of body and spirit as he found them. For one paralyzed man he both restored his body and forgave his sins (Mark 2:3-12). He cared for the whole person. So should we.

Our goal in giving spiritual care is not to credit ourselves with the number of patients who accept what we believe. We are not trying to proselytize in this sense. Neither do we take advantage of our patients' vulnerability and weakness. Jesus told us to be witnesses to him (Matthew 28). We are to show, in deed and word, the presence of Christ in our lives and trust that God will touch others around us.

6. Conclusion

What can we say, then, about the ethics of spiritual care as Christian nurses? We turn to Cusveller's chapter on the "ethic of responsibility" in which he proposed that nursing's professional responsibility is to foster the well-being of patients as well as possible. We have established that restoring a patient's relationship with God is the ultimate spiritual need. Thus, nurses are responsible for supporting and fostering that relationship. Cusveller identifies levels of authority for nursing's responsibility: the patient, the family, health care institutions, the profession, and society. Above all of these is God himself. We have to answer to him for what we do, especially regarding the well-being of our fellow human beings.

Most of the time Christian nurses can meet the spiritual needs of their patients within the constraints of institutional policy and social expectations. However, there may be times when conflict arises. Because God is the one to whom we finally answer for our care of patients, we can trust him for wisdom and the Spirit's guidance for traversing the conflict–in Jesus' words, being "wise as serpents and innocent as doves" (Matthew 10:16). The Spirit is very creative in opening doors. We should expect and look for that creativity. Sometimes expressing our faith may mean being reprimanded or even dismissed from employment. Jesus' promise to always be with us will sustain us even in such difficulties. On the other hand, when a patient's spiritual needs are met and her or his well-being enhanced, we will find great satisfaction in knowing that God has touched that person through us.

Discussion questions

1. As a Christian how would you respond to the young Hindu mother in the opening vignette when she shows you a picture of her "god"? What spiritual care skills are needed to address this situation ethically?

2. Some would say that individuals create idols when they define god according to their own understanding. Consider the apostle Paul's response to the "altar to an unknown god" in Acts 17: 23-28. While nurses are not evangelists/preachers like Paul was, how might skillful questioning of patients be helpful in providing spiritual care?

3. How have you seen the spiritual needs for love and relatedness, forgiveness, meaning and purpose, and hope expressed in your patients? What assessment skills led you to identify these needs?

4. Do you agree with the writer that being spiritual and personal are fundamentally the same? Why or why not? What two dimensions of spiritual/personal does the author identify? How do they interact with each other?

5. The author defines spiritual care as supporting and restoring a patient's relationship with God. Can we be providing spiritual care unaware that we are doing so? Have we failed to give spiritual care if we see little or no evidence of such a restored relationship?

5

Professional Responsibility in the Patient-Nurse Relationship

Kees Kleingeld

Vignette

Visiting nurses attend to a young patient with an asthmatic condition at home. The nurses pay serious attention to his care. They help him with new medications, they sit with him during anxious hours, and they take part in the meetings his parents have with physicians. At times his behavior is rude and inappropriate, yet his parents do not seem to correct him. The nurses wonder if they have a responsibility to "teach the kid some manners" or at least to give his parents some advice on disciplining children.

1. The relationship between nurses and patients

1.1 Introduction

The foregoing chapters gave us insight into the characteristic grounds and features of the professional responsibility of nurses. In this chapter, we will consider this responsibility with regard to the relationship between nurses and patients. Patients carry the principal responsibility for their own health. The question here is how this responsibility is related to the professional responsibility of nurses.

In their relationship to patients, nurses have at least the following three central duties:
- Practical nursing care,
- Accompaniment,
- Representation.

The primary duty of nurses is the performance of practical care for the patients' benefit. Secondly, they offer patients empathy, consolation, attention, and recognition of their feelings. We sometimes call this the "therapeutic function" of the nurse. A third nursing duty is the promotion of the patients' interests by being their spokesperson in interdisciplinary consultation, extended family discussions, and so on.

We may use several metaphors and models to explain the relationship between the personal responsibility of patients and the professional responsibility of nurses.[1] In the next paragraphs three models are considered with a view to seeing whether any one of them can be used to clarify nurses' professional responsibility, while using their three central duties regarding patients as reference points. We recognize recent metaphors like the nurse as partner in a business transaction, the nurse as patient advocate, and the nurse as representative of a bureaucratic organization. In addition, we recognize traditional metaphors like the nurse as part of a military hierarchy, as handmaid in the temple of healing, and as caring mother. All of these images highlight relevant aspects of nurses' responsibility and are worth examining. For present purposes, however, the focus is on the perennial images of the nurse
- as caring mother,
- as business exchange partner,
- as patient advocate.

1.2 The caring mother

The traditional picture of the nurse is that of a caring mother.[2] Even within the nursing profession itself this image is sometimes still defended: "nursing is nurturing and caring for someone in a motherly fashion."[3] As long as patients are not able to administer drugs or prescribe treatments to themselves, as long as they cannot attend to their physical or mental needs,

---

[1] The older articles mentioned in this section are also available in Pence, T. and Cantrall J. eds. *Ethics in Nursing: An anthology.* New York: National League for Nursing, 1990.

[2] Or the "Gentle Sister, the highly skilled but sweetly submissive nurse of tradition." Newton, L.H. "A Vindication of the Gentle Sister: Comment on 'The Fractured Image.'" Eds. Spicker, S.F. and Gadow, S. *Nursing, Images and Ideals.* New York: Springer, 1980. 35.

[3] Wiedenbach, E. in George, J.B. ed. *Nursing Theories.* East Norwalk: Appleton & Lange, 1990[3]. 165.

someone else has to perform these tasks. All sorts of assistance in daily activities, such as dressing and undressing, are needed; the same kind of assistance a mother gives to her children. Secondly, in the somewhat frightening hospital environment and the even more frightening situation of being severely ill, so the metaphor suggests, patients seek "motherly consolation." In other words, they need a surrogate-mother. Lisa Newton even states that this role is both feasible and necessary, for "in a sterile world of authoritative professionals, only the humble, obedient nurse seems to be operating anywhere near the patient's level; she is not a threat because she's in the same boat."[4] Thirdly, just like caring mothers in the family, nurses look after the members of the hospital's family, not only the patients but also the physicians who assume the father's role, according to this model. Newton sketches the hospital as a moral monstrosity. Consequently, nurses are necessary to make the system morally tolerable.[5]

What about this image? On the positive side, we see that the model of the caring mother accentuates the practical and caring aspects of nurses' professional responsibility. It also does justice to the therapeutic aspects of the nursing relation, i.e., supporting and comforting the patient. However, the role of "surrogate mother" is not altogether appropriate for professional nurses. In this model, the boundaries of the nurses' responsibility are blurred. Anything done out of benevolence could be permitted. The patients' own responsibilities for their health and behavior are overshadowed. And certainly a decisive objection against this image, as Newton uses it, is that it is merely a justification for a possibly monstrous system. It is an open question whether this picture does justice to the average hospital. But more importantly, this model derives the professional responsibility of nurses from certain features of the hospital system, thus denying them an independent responsibility for the health and well-being of patients. In our analysis this model cannot be correct.

1.3 The nursing contract

In the Dutch situation, and probably in many more besides, the relationship between caregivers and patients is sometimes described as a sort of contract, suggesting that the practice of care takes place in a market ruled by supply and demand. In that image, medical and nursing care are merely services, offered for fee to people who want to avail themselves of care, in the same way they avail themselves of a car or the services of a

---

[4] Newton 1980, 40.
[5] Newton, L.H. "In Defence of the Traditional Nurse." *Nursing Outlook* 29 (June 1981): 348-354.

plumber. In this manner, for instance, physicians may offer annual examinations to those who can afford them. But also other facilities, such as home care, are regulated by supply and demand.

In this line of thought, the need arises for formal contracts as a means to establish a caring relation. Therefore, the relationship between caregivers, including nurses, and their patients is basically a relationship between service providers and consumers. Being a patient is being a consumer, able to reason as consumers do. This image of health care opens up an emancipatory perspective for the citizens of our modern societies. The assumption is that caring can be based on a relationship of equality and autonomy between nurses and patients, who are able to choose intelligently from a variety of services. "Nowadays we are in the first place consumers," says Dutch philosopher Rob Houtepen. "In this regard, physician and patient have no special relationship and neither does the physician have a special role in the patient's experience concerning health and sickness."[6] Even if we do not like to put caring relationships in terms of a marketplace, we can understand the need to document treatment plans in writing—relationships between caregivers and patients are indeed becoming more and more impersonal.

And so it is for nurses, some say. They point to the plausibility or even desirability of describing nurses' responsibility for patient care in terms of contracts (agreements about the delivery of care) or at least of comparing it to a contract. This understanding entails the view that patients are free to define their relationship to nurses.[7] Nurses are contractually committed to provide the nursing care agreed to with the patient. On this view, a contract provides protection to both nurses and patients and clearly defines their relationship. The extent and the intent of the care required is laid down in a contract, as well as limiting conditions (such as certain things a patient definitively does not wish), perhaps on the basis of a moral or religious commitment.

So perhaps this model has something going for it. What else is to be said? First, there is an assumption that patients are capable of determining and defending their own interests. (Something is in a person's interest if it increases his opportunities to get what he needs. It is in his best interest to take ideals and long-term results into account. It is in my interest not to

---

[6] Houtepen, R. "Deskundigheid met mate." ["Expertise in good measure"] *Scripta Medico-Philosophica* (1990) 7, 19-30. See for the same train of thought, albeit from a different starting point, Sade, R. "Medical Care as a Right: A refutation." *New England Journal of Medicine* 285 (1971): 1288-1292.

[7] Smith, S. "Three Models of the Nurse-Patient Relation." Spicker and Gadow 1980, 176-188. The quote is on page 183.

have pain. It is also in my best interest to visit the dentist.) This right also assumes that patients' ability to judge their interests and to make decisions is not impaired by their illness or hospitalization. The contract image of the nurse-patient relation, therefore, is best understood as a response to paternalism, to lack of commitment and compassion on the side of caregivers, to fear of violations of patients' autonomy, and perhaps to fear of legal liability in those cases.

In regard to paternalism, however, this model risks tipping the scales the other way to where patients' demands and wishes are considered decisive in all nurses' decision-making. That would make other considerations irrelevant, even those based on expertise, solid information, and common sense. In a pluralist society, all kinds of requested care can be contracted, irrespective of their rightness or absurdity. Not only would we then lose all grounds for professional arguments to care in a specific way for specific patients,[8] we would then have arrived at pure consumerism. The contract model is based on an idealization of modern society as one consisting of adult, independent, and reasonable individuals. Yet when persons are capable of arranging contracts, they won't usually be in need of care; and when they are in need of care, they won't usually be capable of negotiating contracts. It is unrealistic to assume that contracts to obtain medical or nursing care can be entered into by, say, demented elderly people or by disabled newborns.

Admittedly, the contract model can accommodate the three central duties of nursing responsibility mentioned above: practical care, accompaniment, and representation. If recorded, contracts give both caregivers and patients legal safeguards against negligence, therapeutic obstinacy, or abuse. Then again, the contract model of the caring relationship suggests that nurses have no professional responsibility unless there is an explicit agreement. But the question is whether a safeguard against legal liability does justice to the rich texture of the mutual moral responsibilities of those involved. Under a contract, caregivers might be allowed to omit actions necessary for the well-being of their patients because these actions were not part of the contract. And, the other way around, contracted interventions may take place, even if they have lost their point. This is a genuine risk in health care, where the person requiring care is usually in an inferior position. In most health care facilities, the contracting parties would seldom be on a par. So in a way, the contract model is based on a lack of trust between patients and caregivers: "I must try to guarantee that I get what I have a

---

[8] Kikuchi, J.F. "Multicultural Ethics in Nursing Education: A potential threat to responsible practice." *Journal of Professional Nursing* 12.3 (1996): 159-165.

right to," so the patient thinks, and "I only do what I am required to do," thinks the nurse. But isn't it precisely the disparity between both parties that calls for nurses to assume responsibility for their patients? And likewise, given this essential disparity, isn't trust essential for the nurse-patient relation? (see Chapter III).

There is yet another objection to the contract model. Contracts belong to the world of economics. The introduction of the contract model in health care harbors the risk that health care be seen as a product with a certain price. When the capacity to produce is limited, however, prices rise and the ability to purchase becomes the prerogative of those who can afford it.[9] Moreover, if health care institutions are inclined to think in terms of products and even profits, their main concern will not be the treatment of patients, but the achievement of production targets. This soil for commercial and industrial exploitation of health care may cause some serious injustices. People who cannot afford to pay for health care will be excluded from the care they need, whereas others could buy more than they need. Furthermore, care that does not produce enough in terms of money or results will not be delivered anymore, which would exclude certain categories of "unprofitable" patients from much needed treatments, such as those with chronic conditions.

1.4 Patient Advocacy

In the United States, and elsewhere, nurses' professional responsibility has led to a view of the nurse as a "Patient Advocate" (PA). Some have argued that patients feel estranged in the complex world of health care. This need gives root to a call for protection against the domination of the medical technology and hospital bureaucracy, which tends to neglect the patients' need for care.

It is clear that serving patients' interests and representing them when they are unable to represent themselves is an aspect of nursing responsibility. And for nurses to see it as part of their duty to have their patients' interests at heart comes close to the advocate model. But what do we mean by "advocate" in this context? That meaning is not clear at all. *Webster's New World Dictionary* defines the meaning of *advocate* as follows:

- one who pleads the cause of another in a court of law; a counsel or counselor;
- one who defends, vindicates, or espouses a cause by argument;

---

[9] See Sade 1971.

- one who is a friend to the oppressed, an upholder of rights, or defender of peace.

With this in mind, it is clear that a PA may serve the interests of patients in different ways. In this section, we discuss three different kinds of advocate:

- The legal rights advocate,
- The moral rights advocate, and
- The existential advocate of the patient.

Legal Rights

Annas and Healey describe the classical vindication of the patients' rights advocate (in short: PRA).[10] They present a juridical interpretation of the task of the patient's advocate. The task of the PRA is, first of all, to support patients and their families as they gain information in order to establish what their interests are so as to be able to promote them. This may involve different treatment options, second opinions, disclosure of medical records, and so on. The PRA may seek to defend the patients' rights, such as the right to adequate information about proposed medical treatments, the right to refuse or accept a treatment, the right to information about diagnosis and prognosis, and so on.

Annas and Healey use the word *right* as a synonym for *personal interest*. In the relationship between physicians and patients they discern four interests, formulated as rights:

- The right to the whole truth,
- The right to privacy and personal dignity,
- The right to retain self-determination by participation in the making of decisions regarding one's health care,
- The right to complete access to medical records both during and after the hospital stay.

While meant to provide guidance for the patient-caregiver relationship, these rights often give rise to conflicts of interest between patients and physicians. When this happens, patients need a competent advocate, who ensures:

- Protection of patients against institutional bureaucracy,
- Participation of patients as partners in their own personal health care programs,
- A balanced view of the appropriateness of modern medical technology and pharmaceuticals;

---

[10] Annas, G.J. and Healey, J. "The Patient Rights Advocate." *Journal of Nursing Administration* 4 (May-June, 1974): 25-31.

61

- Promotion of a humane death and prevention of senseless postpone-
ment of death.

To act as a good PRA, independence vis-à-vis physicians and medical institutions is needed. Despite several counterarguments, Annas is convinced
that nurses are best suited to fulfill this role, provided they are given the
right education. Their experience and their knowledge of hospital administration, as well as medicine and medical terminology provide the perfect
background for a PRA.[11] Their contacts with patients are more frequent
and, because of their lower rank in the hospital hierarchy, closer to the patients' experience.

One of those counterarguments is that nurses have insufficient knowledge of the law, juridical jargon, and societal relations. In addition, they are
said to lack sufficient psychological insight and are not trained to interview
patients. According to Annas, however, it is easier for nurses to acquire this
other knowledge than for others to acquire knowledge of nursing. Another
counterargument is that—in the eyes of the public and the media—nurses are
still seen as the physician's handmaiden, which would hamper patients' trust
in their role as strong advocates. Annas states that better nursing education
will help to overcome these problems.

In the meantime we have drifted rather far away from nurses' central duties of delivering care and supporting patients. Even if nursing education
and experience is required for a PRA, it is clear that the responsibility of a
PRA is not the same as the responsibility of nurses. As Annas and Healey
see it, the PRA's only duty is representation and provision of information.
They assume, furthermore, that the patients' autonomy (secured by the
PRA) is paramount, and at all times patients determine what is in their best
interest, rather than the nurses' therapeutic expertise and comforting presence. Thus, a large part of the nurse's professional responsibility is ignored,
e.g. caring for people whose self-support is in some aspect insufficient. It
comes as no surprise then, that many hospitals employ PRA's who are not
per se nurses; in some hospitals they are social-workers, in others ethicists or
lawyers.

Moral Rights

In most countries, the government has the explicit duty to promote public health. The right to health care is one of the rights of citizens commonly
acknowledged in these countries. Therefore, the right to life and the right to
health care represent justified claims that everyone should respect and sup-

---

[11] Annas, G.J. "The Patient Rights Advocate: Can nurses effectively fill the role?" *Supervisor
Nurse* 5 (July 1974): 20-23, 25.

port citizens' abilities to live as human beings. According to Bandman and Bandman, these moral rights–together with the right to protection from injury–are at the basis of the nurse's professional responsibility.[12] On this account, patients have their rights, whether formulated as wishes and wants or as their best interests. It is sometimes necessary, however, to delegate the exercise of these rights to others such as nurses, who then act in the patient's best interest. This form of paternalism would be justified when patients are in such poor condition that they no longer are free to exercise certain rights. The promotion of moral rights by nurses, defending the patient's needs, amounts to the duties of a patient advocate. According to Bandman and Bandman, "patient advocacy by nurses is essential to patients' health care rights."

Surely, Bandman and Bandman are pointing to an important aspect of nurses' responsibility, but not to the whole of it. They put patient care in the center and include the promotion of the patient's interests. In their opinion, the nurse as advocate is an accurate model, even though many others use the same label in many different ways. Using it for the responsibility Bandman and Bandman have in mind, however, will be courting confusion.

Existential Advocacy

For Sally Gadow,[13] Existential Advocacy (EA) provides both patients and nurses with a means to model their relationship according to their own outlook: one as parent and child, as client and adviser, friend and friend, and so on. EA is an attempt to help patients clarify what they themselves want in their particular situation. This role implies that it is necessary for nurses to gain insight into the situation and capacities of the patient and understand his norms and values. Hence, nurses take part in patients' attempts to clarify the meaning they experience in illness, suffering, and death.

In her own, more technical language, Gadow makes a distinction between the lived body and the object body. The lived body is the body that I am acquainted with in my actions. It is the body that I am; it is I, so to speak. The object body is the body that I experience as something other, distinct from my self. It is the body that I have. Disease and illness, for instance, make me aware of my object body. In that situation, I experience a discrepancy between my lived body and my object body; my own body becomes alien to me. That body is the object of medical or physical examination. The experience of inca-

---

[12] Bandman, B. and Bandman, E. "The Nurse's Role in an Interest-Based View of Patients' Rights." Spicker and Gadow 1980, 125-147.
[13] Gadow, S. "Existential Advocacy: Philosophical foundation of nursing." Spicker and Gadow 1980, 79-101.

pacity is one of the first things patients experience in cases of illness or disability. With EA, so Gadow argues, it is the nurse's responsibility to assist the incapacitated individual, the patient, to experience the body's "object-ness" as his or her own lived body again, rather than allowing it to remain alien.[14]

Gadow's argument is colored by her own philosophy. Her leading principle is the unlimited self-care or independent "self-determination" of patients. This is not the kind of self-care we meet in the self-care deficit theory of Dorothea Orem. Rather, it "refers to actions personally selected and initiated, and thus freely performed by an individual in the interest of promoting that person's health as he or she construes it."[15] The principle of "self-care" assumes full mental competence of patients. This betrays an anthropology that is *de facto* incorrect and *de jure* undesirable. People are seldom if ever fully independent and competent, especially in times of illness and disease, nor should they be treated as such. In addition, a nurse who starts from Gadow's humanistic philosophy and concepts risks imposing her underlying values upon their patients. If she does, then her very role as EA will restrict the patient's autonomy! To say the least, then, Gadow's concept of nurses' professional responsibility poses a problem for anyone who does not accept her philosophical foundations (and a paradox to anyone who does). For interpreting nurses' responsibility as EA requires the acceptance of a philosophy that is in conflict with our beliefs about the nature of being human and the nature of nursing care.

Lastly, another question is whether nurses really are such chameleons that they can practice EA with different sorts of patients. Most of the existential or spiritual questions a patient has (for instance, his troubles regarding the meaning of life or his outlook on relations) seem to belong to the realm of pastoral work or counseling. At any rate, the existential "self-care" propagated by Gadow as the core of nurses' professional responsibility, suggests that patients themselves would choose their EA, but the latter would not necessarily have to be a nurse! Should nurses see the exercise of EA as the core of their professional responsibility, they adopt a self-defeating position.[16] (See Chapter IX on alternative therapies for a practical example of the problems generated by EA.)

---

[14] Gadow 1980, 93-96.

[15] Gadow, S. "Allocating Autonomy: Can patients and practitioners share?" *Who Decides? Conflicts of rights in health care.* Ed. Bell N.K. Clifton: Humana, 1982, 96.

[16] Bishop A.H. and Scudder, J.D. *The Practical, Moral and Personal Sense of Nursing.* Albany: SUNY, 1990, 22-27.

2. Autonomy and paternalism

In health care (or at least the ethics and law of health care), the word "autonomy" is frequently heard, often in combination with "paternalism" as its counterpart. They are both foundational, as we have seen, to the texture of responsibilities between nurses and patients. Before we evaluate the aforementioned models of nurses' professional responsibility in relation to patients, it will be helpful to examine further the concepts of autonomy and paternalism.

2.1 Autonomy

The concept of autonomy has been used in a large variety of ways. It can mean that one is one's own master who is free to act and choose and do what one wants. If autonomy is a right, it is a cultural right, one that must be learned. Often the meaning of the concept is specified by contrasting autonomy and heteronomy. This contrast may lead to a misconception, for it suggests that autonomy is laying down one's own law. This definition is too narrow a concept of autonomy but one that is typical for modern society. It is sometimes suggested that heteronomy excludes freedom of choice. However, when we see ourselves as heteronymous in the sense of regulating our conduct by what God's law asks from us, that concept leaves more than enough room for freedom of choice. This type of heteronomy is sometimes called theonomy.

Within health care, autonomy mainly refers to patients' autonomy. In our understanding of professional responsibility, though, professional nurses too possess a certain autonomy. Essential for autonomy are independent decision-making and the ability to execute decisions, resulting in an act (including acts of omission). Such an action has the following characteristics:

- The act is rational, i.e., it is executed after weighing reasons;
- The act is voluntary, i.e., the actor is competent;
- The act is authentic, i.e., it is a personal expression of the individual's freedom.

Clearly, not only patients have such autonomy; the nursing role entails a professional autonomy. Furthermore, it is not only professionals who can be paternalistic; there are many others who expose paternalistic behavior in health care as well (think of relatives, or church community representatives). Nevertheless, in this chapter the focus is on the autonomy of patients and the paternalism of professionals.

2.2 A Patient's autonomy

Generally speaking, a patient is someone who notices, "I am ill." His being ill is ordinarily not the result of his own choice; the condition has happened to him. As a patient, the ill person functions differently from before–not only in his physical abilities, but also his assessment of his situation. He often needs help, therefore, in adjusting his affected functions to his daily life or, the other way around, his daily life to his affected functions. Bearing in mind the characteristics of autonomy, we must conclude that a patient is not always a fully autonomous person. His autonomy may be restricted because of

- lack of knowledge,
- lack of possible choices,
- lack of ability.

First, patients often lack the necessary knowledge and insight to assess their own situation. Their state of mind does not always allow them to weigh the different possibilities. The information they have received to give "informed consent" might not be properly appreciated because they lack a medical background. Also, sometimes patients' mental state does not allow them to judge their situations realistically due to confusion, shock, depression, or anxiety.

Secondly, some patients are able to decide and take actions voluntarily relating to their health (for instance, to keep a diet). Other times, however, patients cannot take the actions necessary for recovery of health, precisely because they are ill. Appendicitis patients cannot perform surgery on themselves, severely mentally ill persons cannot medicate themselves properly, and even a simple flu keeps patients from going to the drug store themselves. In these cases, their only choice is between enlisting others to help them and getting no help at all. And even when they choose to accept help, they cannot always freely choose who will provide the appropriate care. The number of persons with the required skills may be limited (think of surgeons) or the facilities at the institution in question may be limited. It is clear that freedom of action is limited here.

When speaking of these "external restrictions" on freedom, we may also discern "internal restrictions." It is not only lack of information or alternatives that may restrict choices. The very fact of being a patient may restrict one's ability to decide and cast doubt on the competence of the patient. The patient may have too rosy or too dark a view of his chances of recovery–and could perhaps need some assistance in this outlook.

Hence, an appeal to patients' autonomy (as a basis for their relationship to nurses) is often not justified. A patient has limited possibilities and is alienated by being ill and needing help. He is not able to organize or control his own healing process. These realities should make us cautious in propagating models of nurses' professional responsibility that view patients as autonomous individuals.

2.3 Paternalism

Do these views on the concept of patient autonomy inevitably lead us into the trap of paternalism? Paternalism here means that the nurses' professional responsibility is to assume the traditional role that a father (Latin, *pater*) or parent has vis-à-vis a child.[17] A parent may send a child to bed, make her eat, or force her to take medicines. Sometimes a parent even "manipulates" a child by telling him a half-lie and then justifying it as in his best interests. The assumption is that children lack the capacity to decide for themselves what is in their own best interests. As soon as a child has this capacity, parental interference would not be justified. Hence, parental intervention is justified if and when

- it is reasonably clear that the result will be in the child's interest;
- the child is unable to judge the impact of the necessary actions and his own long-term interests;
- it is reasonable to assume that the children will endorse the parents' decisions at a later date when they can understand their parents' reasoning.[18]

It is noteworthy that relationships between adults can also have paternalistic traits. For instance, when experts try to force their opinion upon other persons, thinking: "I know best what's in your interest." Generally, paternalism is rejected these days by the appeal to a person's autonomy. In the case of patients, however, we are often dealing with diminished autonomy, as we have seen. Then the delivery of good care may be an argument for some form of paternalistic intervention. But to what extent is this true?

Paternalism properly understood is always linked to good intentions or best interests. We speak of paternalism when an intervention fails to meet the patient's immediate desires but is carried out with a view to serve what is good for him, or what professionals see as such. While this decision may be justified, our understanding of the patient's best interest is sometimes nothing more than a rationalization based on research or institutional policy. So, paternalistic conduct should not to be taken lightly by health care professionals.

---

[17] Martin Benjamin and Joy Curtis correctly use the term "parentalism," but for the sake of convention we shall use *paternalism*. See Benjamin, M. and Curtis, J. *Ethics in Nursing*. New York: Oxford University, 1992[3].

[18] Benjamin and Curtis 1992, 54-55.

In order for paternalistic behavior on the part of nurses to be justified, Benjamin and Curtis point to the following conditions:

- The patient is, under the circumstances, ignorant of relevant information, or his capacity for rational reflection is significantly impaired;
- The patient is likely to be significantly harmed unless the intervention takes place;
- It is reasonable to assume that the patient will, at a later time, with greater knowledge or after recovery, endorse the decision to interfere.[19]

It is clear that the last condition is never met in the case of incompetent patients. In these cases, informed consent is usually replaced by "proxy consent," i.e., permission given on behalf of the patient by some legal representative, such as parents (in the case of children) or children (in the case of elderly). To make proxy consent permissible, certain conditions must be fulfilled, like family ties to the patient, incompetence on the part of the patient, and preferably an assignment of proxy consent to the family written by the patient. It is part of nurses' professional responsibility to know the legislation in his or her country on this point. For instance, if a teenager is pregnant, do you know who has the right to decide that she have an abortion in your country? Do you treat the pregnant teenager as *only* 15 or as *already* 15?

2.4 Evaluation

In the present chapter we have been speaking about the relationship between patients' own responsibility and nurses' professional responsibility. Thus we set out to evaluate a number of metaphors and models of professional responsibility and dug a little deeper into the underlying notions of autonomy and paternalism. Now we can begin our final evaluation of those models.

None of them fully encompasses the various responsibilities of nurses. Traditional metaphors, as we have seen, mainly rest on the assumption of hierarchy and power. They glean nurses' responsibility from the authority of others; they are the humble servants of the physician. We rejected this picture because nurses have a professional responsibility not derived from someone else's professional responsibility. It also gives the wrong content to nurses' responsibility, as it suggests they are "to mother" over the patient, to treat him in an essentially paternalistic way. And this role, as we saw, doesn't acknowledge the patient's own responsibilities for his own life and health.

---

[19] Benjamin and Curtis 1992, 58.

An approach in which the professional responsibility of the nurse is laid down in contractual rights and duties lacks the moral core of the nurse-patient relationship. Nurses are not simply mechanics, offering technical solutions for the repair of malfunctioning bodies. They are basically people meeting the needs of fellow people. The delivery of care sometimes requires moral qualities (such as going the extra mile) that cannot be part of a contract. The relationship between nurses and patients is not like two autonomous contracting parties negotiating to secure their own interests, but it is a relationship of taking care of the other.

Existential Advocacy (Gadow) is not an acceptable alternative. We already mentioned some arguments against it. It imposes a philosophy on others, and it assumes too much responsibility with too narrow a base. It also presupposes that humans are autonomous beings in the sense of laying down their own laws. This concept of autonomy is contrary to the conviction that human autonomy is limited by external and internal restrictions and, above all, by God's law. An additional defect in this model is that it only allots autonomy to patients. What really happens is that patients are confronted by nurses' professional autonomy.

None of this criticism alters the fact that advocacy and mediation belong to nurses' professional responsibility. To this extent the advocate metaphor is correct. But it does not capture the core of nursing responsibility. Advocacy is a part of nursing care. The juridical version of the metaphor—the Patient Rights Advocate—in particular obscures central characteristics of nursing. It is significant that actual PRAs do not in general appear to be nurses. Furthermore, the model of Patient Advocate, and especially that of PRA, suggests confrontation: patients and nurses against the others. That antagonism is not consistent with reality. Of course, sometimes patients are confronted with anonymous and indifferent forces in the modern medical center with its impersonal procedures and highly skilled "technicians." In that environment, nurses may indeed add a humane touch. They may indeed have the required skills and knowledge to find their way through the maze of bureaucracy and to appeal to the technicians in the right way. Nevertheless, all this does not yet adequately describe all the duties and responsibilities of nurses.

On reflection, a value-based metaphor like Gadow's EA is a creed rather than anything else. Only the patients' advocate model, as Bandman and Bandman see it, appears to account adequately for central traits of the nurse's professional responsibility. The problem remains, however, that most of it is only applicable to competent patients.

Autonomy and paternalism, correctly understood, are not mutually exclusive alternatives. Hence, we need not choose between them. In the case of real relationships in caring practices, nurses and patients have their own related responsibilities. Models and metaphors of nurses' professional responsibility must be governed by respect for patients as fellow humans and by trust in nurses as experts who primarily have patients' health interests in mind. We will not propose a metaphor of our own. But in the next section we shall briefly indicate our own views concerning nurses' professional responsibility in relation to patients.

3. Nurses' professional responsibility

3.1 Introduction

Providing "good care" is the purpose of nursing practice. To define "good care," however, is difficult; we would need a philosophical anthropology, and that is beyond the scope of this book. For now, it suffices to mention that we may discern several interrelated dimensions in the human person; there are corporal, relational, social, psychical, ethical, and religious dimensions to being human.[20]

What is good for this patient? To answer this question is the primary task of nursing. This question differs from: "How can I heal this disease?" Nurses, in their encounter with patients, are responsible for the care of persons in all of their dimensions. Their responsibility concerns what we could call activities of daily life, but understood broadly as "care for one's human existence." This care defines the core of nurses' professional responsibility. Indeed, there are other responsibilities (such as advocacy and implementation of evidential support). But they are secondary in that they contribute to the primary responsibility, i.e., the delivery of good care.

Typically, the professional responsibility of nurses comes to the fore in
- their own actions in regard to patients;
- their relationship to the actions of other professionals in regard to patients;
- creating the right conditions for professional practice;
- dealing with patients' relatives.

We will pay closer attention to each of these aspects.

---

[20] I am assuming an anthropology in the Reformed tradition of Christian thought. For details and introduction see Dooyeweerd, H. *A New Critique of Theoretical Thought*, 4 vols. Amsterdam/Philadelphia: Presbyterian and Reformed, 1969 ff.; Troost, A. *The Christian Ethos*. Bloemfontein: Patmos, 1983.

3.2 Nurses' conduct concerning patients

We have mentioned that patients are not always active and competent because they are ill and in need for care. Consequently, they are not able to organize their own treatment and care. In this situation of physical and mental helplessness and dependence, patients are in need of someone who can act on their behalf and accompany and inform them, for the sake of their well-being and health. It is here that we find the primary responsibility of nurses.

How this responsibility is realized depends on the patient's situation. Coordination and information do not mean the same for adults as for children. Furthermore, there are differences between competent and incompetent patients, such as comatose or demented persons. Especially in the case of fully or partially incompetent patients, nurses should ensure that no decisions are made about treatment and care contrary to the interests and rights of the patients. For it is nurses' primary responsibility to do well to patients by trying to overcome or alleviate the consequences of illness, handicap, or medical treatment. The primary raison d'etre of nursing practice remains the care nurses owe patients as human beings. Cutting a patient's toenails and brushing his teeth are not to be omitted as being of lesser importance in a busy unit.

3.3 Other professionals' actions concerning the patient

Usually, patients are surrounded by multiple health professionals rendering help, cure, or care: physicians, physiotherapists, laboratory workers, the list goes on and on. They all have their own specific fields of skill and knowledge, within which they exercise their specific responsibility, derived from the authority associated with their expertise and function (i.e., functional authority). Their skills mainly concern the treatment of patients' diseases and the consequences of the patients' failing abilities. Nurses focus on the consequences of failing abilities for the patients' daily life. In doing so, nurses normally work in conjunction with other professionals providing help to the same patient. Hence, apart from their primary responsibility to deliver direct patient care, nurses have an additional responsibility to mediate. Since nurses are present 24 hours a day, their assistance to others who help their patients is a part of their responsibility. To be sure, this duty will concern the coordination and fine-tuning of help offered by different professionals, not the very content of this assistance. For in that area, the other professional retains his own functional authority and responsibility (see also Chapter VII).

In practice, this differentiation is not self-evident. Often it would appear that some professionals not only assume functional authority but also a hierarchical authority over nurses. This "air" is reflected in the behavior of many physicians in their relationship to patients as well. Of course, physi-

71

cians are responsible for the medical accuracy of their treatment. However, it is the nurses' responsibility to prevent, ease, or relieve uncomfortable consequences of medical treatment in the patient's life. Physicians who claim this responsibility for themselves claim an authority over nurses that they do not have on the basis of their role as medical experts. Sometimes, even various paramedics or nonmedics illegitimately assume authority over nursing staff. In addition, these professionals sometimes undertake tasks or parts of tasks that properly belong to nurses' professional responsibilities. An example would be a grade school tutor on the pediatric unit giving all kinds of instructions to nurses concerning child care, even concerning things nurses have more training in. If nurses are to meet the demands of their profession and do what patients might rightly expect and have a right to, then nurses have to accept their responsibility. If anything, this level of responsibility is the challenge for nurses striving for professionalism.

3.4 Creating conditions for professional conduct

Hospitals and other facilities for health care offer the necessary institutional conditions for the practice of nursing. They are organizations with a management, with tactical and strategic decision-making mechanisms for the execution of decisions that maintain or, if possible, improve professional practice. The creation of conditions for the delivery of care is part of the responsibility of the institution's management when the professionals cannot do this task themselves. This provision takes place, necessarily, within financial limits that are often set from outside (for instance, by government). Thus, the allocation of resources as well as managerial decision-making affect the conditions for nursing practice and have an impact on the freedom of action of nursing staff.

Nurses need a certain amount of space to make independent decisions and act accordingly, based on their expertise and aimed at the patient's well-being and health. This need arises from their professional responsibility. The extent of their authority depends on various circumstances. Looking at the clinical situation, nursing staff is often limited by hospital regulations, medical regimes, or health care politics. When nurses are confronted with consequences of the choices of others in the exercise of their profession, they may not be able to carry out their responsibility. If the nursing staff is involved in decision-making at the level of the institution's management, then they are accountable for the choices made and the results gained. In their everyday practice they may bear responsibility for the choices made. But without participation in and responsibility for policy and decision-making, it is very difficult for nurses to assume full professional responsibility for their work.

Mutatis mutandis, these principles also apply for nursing outside the clinical context, such as home and community care. Sometimes, cutbacks in resources and the increased demands of efficiency make it almost impossible for nurses in many countries to practice their profession in a responsible way. In many countries, for instance, home care is confronted with limited money and personnel. Consequently, providing good care is sometimes out of the question. Can it be justifiable that a patient gets the same care five times a day from five different persons? One thing that can help avoid these problems is giving nurses a voice in the management of the organization in which they are employed.

3.5 Nurses and patients' relatives

Not only do nurses deal with patients, but also with the patients' relatives, especially in children's wards and with incompetent patients. Nevertheless, the main task of nurses is to take care of patients. Their professional responsibility for relatives is restricted to matters directly related to the health and well-being of patients (see also Chapter VII). In all cases but one, internal family problems are outside the scope of nurses' professional responsibility (of course observation, discussion, and referral to an expert may be in order). The only case in which this is not true would be the psychiatric nurse who cares for a "social system," e.g., a family or married couple. Generally speaking, however, children's education is outside the scope of nursing children since nurses are not family therapists. Even with good intentions, nurses must take care not to get involved in such matters.

Here we see important differences between clinical and nonclinical settings. A nurse may offer advice to friends and relatives that would be inappropriate to offer to patients, as with mentally handicapped children. The scope of a nurse's professional responsibility is limited, and we must not lose sight of those limits. Again, certain nurses may have strong health-related arguments against child labor in developing countries. However important those may be, it does not belong to their professional responsibility to urge their colleagues to go out and protest against these situations in their capacity as nurses. They may protest as citizens or concerned fellow humans, but not make it a nursing issue.

4. Conclusion

Responsibility is an important human trait. However, responsibility must be manifested. When we say: "The nurse is taking care of the patient," something exciting happens. The nurse performs actions that are part of a practice, belonging to her professional responsibility, expressing her Christian solidarity. We see this combination of expertise and inspiration in Daniel Callahan's definition of care: "Caring can best be understood as a positive emotional and supportive response to the condition and situation of another person, a response whose purpose is to affirm our commitment to their well-being, our willingness to identify with them in their pain and

73

suffering, and our desire to do what we can to relieve their situation."[21] On this understanding, we see care as a manifestation of responsibility. In the caring relation, those who are cared for and those who provide care have their own responsibility. It is part of nurses' professional responsibility to distinguish these two and to act in such a way that both are done justice.

Discussion questions

1. The visiting nurses in the vignette have been called in to attend to the boy's asthmatic conditions. Do you think it is their responsibility to correct the boy's manners? Do you think it is also their responsibility to give the parents advice regarding his education?

2. The author distinguishes three central duties in the nurses' professional responsibility: practical support, social accompaniment, and advocacy. How do these duties help to clarify the visiting nurses' responsibility in the vignette?

3. The author defends the view that promoting patient autonomy is not the chief end of the work nurses do. Do you agree? What would that position mean in the vignette about the asthmatic boy?

4. What do you think the author means to say in the section on paternalism? Would paternalism be appropriate in the case of the asthmatic boy? Or in the care of a pregnant 15-year old?

5. Do you think a Christian nursing ethic is by nature paternalistic? Or against autonomy? Can nurses still uphold a Christian ethic in a pluralistic society?

---

[21] Callahan, D. *What Kind of Life: The limits of medical progress.* New York: Simon and Schuster, 1990, 144.

6

Professional Responsibility in Nurses' Relationships to Colleagues and Their Profession

Fu-Jin Shih

Vignette

Suzy, Kim, and Paul, three staff nurses in a psychiatric hospital, discuss during lunch break how to respond to the new collective labor agreements proposed by their national nurses' union. The union is exerting some pressure to go on strike if these proposals are not accepted in the upcoming negotiations. Suzy, Kim, and Paul all reject the option of a strike to secure better salaries, albeit for different reasons.

Suzy: I think it is always wrong for nurses to go on strike. I believe patients will always suffer during a strike because they are the most vulnerable people involved.

Kim: I agree that a strike is a bad idea, but because a strike is taking a stand against the legitimate governing authorities. To me as a Christian, at least, that seems wrong.

Paul: Well, I'm also looking at it from a Christian perspective. But I think a strike could be justified if no alternatives remain to make clear that we can't do our jobs as nurses properly anymore. In that situation, a strike seems to me to be the only way to promote the well-being of the patient!

How will (and should) Suzy, Kim, and Paul respond when the call to strike actually comes from their union?

1. Introduction

1.1 Aim

This chapter's topic is nurses' professional responsibility in their relationships to colleagues and their profession, and, in particular, how ethical issues in these relationships affect Christian nurses. In their well-known book on nursing ethics, Benjamin and Curtis discuss a number of such issues, analyzing them in terms of the ethical principles and values that are at stake.[1] These situations include cover-up of a colleague's medication errors, judgmental behavior by colleagues, confidentiality and administrative issues regarding a colleague's personal problems affecting his work, and conscientious refusal, e.g., of preferential treatment for certain patients. While showing contextual sensitivity to practical and personal factors influencing cooperation (see also Chapter VII), Benjamin and Curtis always resolve the dilemma in light of nurses' responsibility for the patient's well-being. Unlike Benjamin and Curtis, however, this chapter will concentrate on a few issues that may arise for Christian nurses in particular.

The focus of this chapter is on fostering professional relationships and dialogue among nurses with a view to resolving and even preventing ethical dilemmas, rather than giving an ethical analysis of the dilemmas as such. In addition to the aforementioned issues, we will address those that we deem important to Christian nurses. The aim of the chapter, then, is to provide food for thought regarding the following questions:

- What is the nurse's professional responsibility in relation to other members of her team and their profession?
- What moral dilemmas may nurses expect in regard to their relationships with colleagues and their profession? In particular, what dilemmas may Christian nurses expect, for instance, in situations of disagreement over the care to be provided?[2]
- How can nurses, especially Christian nurses, deal with those dilemmas given their professional responsibility?

Answers to these questions will promote a better understanding of nurses' ethical dilemmas in daily practice. This discussion may help Christian nurses and their colleagues improve their collaboration in order to prevent ethical problems or to manage them at an early stage.

1.2 Context

Nursing leaders—which include nursing educators, administrators, researchers, and clinicians—face many challenges in the twenty-first century. One of the most complex is the lack of internationally accepted theoretical

---

[1] Benjamin, M. and Curtis, J. *Ethics in Nursing.* New York: Oxford University, 1992[3]. 131-158.

[2] For other examples in relation to the profession, see Tschudin, V. *Ethics in Nursing: The caring relationship.* Oxford: Butterworth-Heinemann, 1992[2]. 127-133.

and practical guidelines or protocols for managing the situations in which ethical dilemmas arise. Factors complicating the challenges nurses face include the various "philosophies of nursing" adopted by the profession, society, nursing associations, medical associations, and the general public. Neither can we ignore the mission, vision, and life goals of the individual nurse, including personal values, belief systems, and cultural frameworks. Furthermore, nurses are confronted by differing expectations from the individual's religious affiliation or that of the nursing community, professional association, or general public. And on an institutional level, there are expectations inherent to interpersonal, interinstitutional, and intercultural communication patterns.

In other words, value and belief systems and expectations are fundamental to the decision-making process both of individual nurses and groups of nurses. Hence, ethical issues sometimes require an in-depth contextual and philosophical analysis of the actual situations at hand. Also, the process of discussion often takes a long time, consumes a lot of energy, and is rarely a trouble-free path to consensus. Therefore, the nurse's attention is generally directed to managing the most immediate and conflict-free matters. As a result, it is understandable if ethical issues become of secondary or tertiary priority for nurses. In the present author's experience, accordingly, nurse clinicians, and also nursing educators and administrators, often lack confidence in managing ethical dilemmas.

Moreover, nurse clinicians may find that they are confused about their personal and professional values and, thus, feel uncomfortable about addressing ethical issues. Indeed, some try to avoid ethical issues altogether. As a result, they may miss opportunities to prevent or detect ethical problems at an early stage. We will focus our comments on this stage.

1.3 Outline

The following five situations show the kinds of dilemmas nurses, and especially Christian nurses, may expect to encounter in their relationships with their colleagues and profession:

- situations in which the patient's relatives and friends are involved. Suppose the nurse disagrees with their involvement. If so, what is the nurse's professional responsibility?
- situations that test the nurse's commitment to work with other nurses in order to achieve care of a high quality for patients. How do you work with nurses who fail to uphold professional standards?
- situations in which there is a difference of opinion between colleagues about the importance of providing spiritual care. For example, a Christian nurse taking care of a patient who is interested in the Christian faith may disagree with a colleague of another faith who is reluctant to provide spiritual care for that patient.

77

- situations in which Christian nurses disagree with colleagues on the provision of alternative therapies.
- situations in which Christian nurses are faced with colleagues involved in misconduct such as the stealing of drugs or nursing supplies.

1.4 Some basic elements

We will conclude our introduction with some general principles of professional responsibility related to the nursing profession and to membership of a team. Of course, the nurse's primary professional responsibility is to provide care for the benefit of the patient. This is a moral responsibility (see Chapter II). If something gets in the way of her duty to care, then the nurse faces a moral problem. Furthermore, a nurse seldom provides care for patients on her own. Mostly, she is a member of a team, whose members co-operate to provide care. Thus, the nurse's professional responsibility is a *shared* responsibility. In addition, nursing never takes place in a social vacuum but in an institution providing the conditions for patient care. The fact that the nurse is part of a team, a profession, and an institution has a bearing on the exercise of authority and power. The nurse's professional responsibility, then, involves knowledge and acceptance of the hierarchical infrastructure of the team. Lastly, nurses always work with other people who, like them, deserve what all ordinary human beings deserve, created as they are in God's image. Therefore, general norms of decency and civility also apply to the working relationships of and between nurses.

2. Family involvement

The first kind of dilemma involves disagreement about patients' needs for long-term companionship by their family members. This is an issue in countries where family ties are strong, but not only there. The concept of a "patient system" in the nursing profession is suggested to include patients and their so-called *significant others* (relatives, although they may also include close friends). But there are a number of questions to be answered in this context:

- To what degree should the relatives be involved? In other words, who are the patient's relatives and when or to what extent should nurses involve them in the patient's care?
- How much attention should nurses pay to the patient's relatives themselves?
- To what extent should Christian nurses encourage their colleagues to facilitate a good relationship with patients and their relatives in order to empower the patients' relatives to take care of them after their discharge from the hospital?

These questions are becoming more and more important in many parts of the world, not least in Asia, South America, and many eastern and southern

European regions, where the central unit of society remains the family.[3] To answer questions like these, the background of the dilemma needs to be understood. In some cultures, it is often necessary to give health-related information to the whole family or to key persons in the family. Medical and nursing choices are not usually made by the individual patient or by a single family member, but rather by the patient's whole family. More than one family member may consult health care providers, physicians, and nurses on many different occasions. This involvement has become a challenge for many nurses because their workload is increasing and the quality of care must be maintained, while time is limited. In this case, some nurses become impatient with patients and their family members. If the family proves more appreciative of the approach taken by a Christian nurse compared to her colleagues, a conflict may arise between the Christian nurse and her colleagues whose attitudes are perceived as less friendly.

Important principles for Christians are that human beings are created as social beings and that families play an important role in their flourishing and development. Also sensitivity to humanity's cultural diversity ties in with the Christian worldview. To be sure, social and cultural animosity, group pressure, and oppression (given the reality of sin) should not be underestimated. Nonetheless, part of nurses' professional responsibility involves encouraging the family's support of the patient, in as far as it contributes to his flourishing or well-being.

How should nurses, and in particular Christian nurses, deal with controversy over family involvement, given their professional responsibility? First, Christian nurses may help their colleagues understand relevant legal, cultural, and individual points of view. A person often feels vulnerable when he or she is ill. Patients may request that the relatives identified by them should stay at their bedside for some period of time which, in some cases, could be all day long. The company of relatives may have several advantages. For instance, patients feel more secure when a trusted companion is involved in their care; companionship of family members can create a home-like environment and can decrease the sense of insecurity and discomfort created by an unfamiliar environment. In addition, family members will probably be familiar with the patient's preferences regarding daily activities and may help the patient adjust to the new daily routines in the hospital. Furthermore, family members can provide immediate help when nurses are

---

[3] Shih, F.J. "Taiwanese Patients' Expectation for Recovery from Cardiac Surgery during Admission Transition." *Journal of Nursing Research* (ROC) 3 (1995): 309-322; Shih, F.J. et al. "The Impact of Cadaveric Organ Donation on Taiwanese Donor Families During the First Six Months after Donation." *Psychosomatic Medicine* 63 (2001): 69-78; Shih, F.J. et al. "The Dilemma of 'To-Be or Not-to-Be': Needs and expectations of Taiwanese cadaveric organ donor families during the pre-donation transition." *Social Science and Medicine* (in press).

not immediately available. In practice, family members can serve as important communication liaisons between the patient and health care workers, and are able to provide immediate social and emotional support at critical times when needed. In some cultures, family members are encouraged to take turns accompanying the patient during his stay in hospital. Therefore, the meaning of the relatives' companionship needs to be carefully appraised, taking into consideration different cultural and medical traditions.[4]

Regarding the question of how much attention the patient's relatives deserve in virtue of the nurse's professional responsibility, nurses should encourage their colleagues to foster healthy relationships between patients and their relatives. They can clarify the expectations and the roles of relatives in the hospital, from the patient's, his family's, and other health professionals' perspectives. Christian nurses should also make an effort to help colleagues understand the cultural background and the meaning of a relative's role, and promote consensus regarding expectations about the relative's role. Lastly, nurses may need to facilitate communication between patients, their relatives, and health professionals, and help the relatives learn to take care of the patient in preparation for the patient's discharge from the hospital.[5] By doing so, a supportive relationship can be nurtured and maintained, and a better understanding between nurses, their colleagues, and the "patient systems" would more easily be achieved. (For further discussion of the nurse-patient relationship, also see Chapter V.)

3. Disagreements over quality of care

The second dilemma, from a Christian point of view, is that nurses are sometimes confronted with colleagues who do not seem to be committed to providing care of a high quality. The concept of quality of care in the nursing profession implies care with a view to maintaining or improving the patient's health. Health, according to the World Health Organization definition (of 1998), means physical, psychological, social, and spiritual well-being. For many nurse clinicians, the most understandable and concrete part of this definition is that of physical well-being. Nevertheless, many nurses will also be seeking to promote psychological, social, and spiritual well-being. This desire remains in spite of nurses spending less and less time with patients since the average stay in hospital is becoming shorter in many countries and the nurse to patient ratio is decreasing, mainly for reasons of cost containment. In stressful circumstances like these, good collaboration between disciplines is essential to promote the efficiency and dedication

---

[4] Shih 1995; Shih, F.J. et al. "Taiwanese Patients' Concerns and Coping Strategies: Transition to Cardiac Surgery." *Heart & Lung* 27 (1998): 82-98.

[5] Shih, F.J. "Perceptions of Self in the Intensive Care Unit after Cardiac Surgery among Adult Taiwanese and American-Chinese Patients." *International Journal of Nursing Studies* 34 (1997): 17-26.

needed for good quality care. Good interpersonal relationships between health team members are also crucial for collaboration between disciplines.

Ethical dilemmas often become more complex and difficult if they are confounded by prejudice, distorted value systems, emotional disturbances, or poor interpersonal communication.[6] For example, some nurses may have a preference for or negative attitudes towards a particular socio-economic class or ethnic group. Hence, they may have difficulties in maintaining professional interpersonal relationships with their colleagues or with patients. And so, their motivation to provide good quality care may be diminished, or they may be involved in inappropriate interactions vis-à-vis patients and their family members. In addition, they may badly affect the contributions of their colleagues to the nursing care of the patient and unnecessarily misunderstand their colleagues' decisions. If the patient's well-being is affected by misunderstandings or disagreements, ethical problems may well arise (see also Chapter VII).

Some recommendations may be given to help Christian nurses who confront these kinds of problems. First, Christian nurses may learn to establish interpersonal relationships with their colleagues of the type the Jewish philosopher Martin Buber calls "I - Thou" rather than "I - It."[7] Buber believes that if a person shows the same kind of respect for other people as for God, they will establish healthy interpersonal relationships.

Secondly, nurses are encouraged to engage in honest self-reflection, involving assessment of the beliefs, value systems, and life goals which influence their attitudes toward health and illness, and on which their cultural or ethnic preferences, their ethical framework, and related decision making are founded.[8] Thus it is necessary for nurse educators and leaders to help nursing students and nurse clinicians explore their own personal values and beliefs and to understand the cultural and ethnic backgrounds of patients better in order to prevent prejudice and decisions that are harmful to patients or colleagues.

Finally, in order to accomplish this mutual respect, various effective teaching philosophies and strategies need to be developed and tested. Teaching in the classroom as well as in clinical settings is recommended. Knowledge and appreciation of different ethnic identities and cultures might be stimulated by the following strategies. One option includes lectures and courses on history and major thought-systems of specific cultures. This teaching should enable nurses to appreciate various cultural expres-

---

[6] Shelly, J.A. *Dilemma: A nurse's guide for making ethical decisions.* Downers Grove: InterVarsity, 1980.

[7] Buber, M. *I and Thou.* There is more than one English translation from the German original.

[8] Shih, F.J. "Concepts Related to Chinese Patients' Perceptions of Health, Illness and Person: Issues of Conceptual Clarity." *Accident and Emergency Nursing* 4 (1996): 208-215.

sions of different civilizations. It should include some understanding of their literature, scripture, art, and craft, which can be gained by visiting museums and going to concerts or libraries. Another educational tool might be field trips to other patients' or colleagues' communities or societies, perhaps even involving travel abroad and shared cross-cultural lectures at foreign nursing schools and medical institutes. In a ward-based situation, group discussions of case studies are helpful in understanding the multiple needs and cultural backgrounds of patients; next to that, it might be helpful to actually have duties involving care of patients from different ethnic backgrounds and duties that involve meeting with the patient's family members. On a more interpersonal level, the promotion of interethnic friendships between colleagues may be helpful, and the recruitment of bilingual volunteers to facilitate communication between health professionals, students, and patients, as well as their family members. Those measures should serve to promote openness and humility with a view to learning from one another and promoting communication among colleagues that involves mutual respect and support. The human dignity of colleagues and patients as well as their "significant others" from different cultures should always be kept in mind.

4. Religious diversity in team and profession

4.1 Disagreement over spiritual care

The third dilemma that Christian nurses may frequently experience relates to situations in which they are caring for patients who have a growing interest in the Gospel, while working with nonbelieving colleagues who are hesitant to provide spiritual care. What should the Christian nurse do? Some step-by-step strategies may be suggested to help Christian nurses motivate patients to ask for the Lord's healing help in their health-related difficulties.

Dilemmas of this sort can involve some infringement on what is seen as the patient's well-being. Part of the disagreement centers on what counts as the patient's well-being. Christian commitment brings with it a perspective on human flourishing which includes spiritual well-being defined as a dynamic personal relationship with God.[9] Nurses with different commitments may not see well-being this way. So controversy arises over not only the actualization of nurses' responsibility, but even over what their responsibility *is*: fostering spiritual well-being or not? (see also Chapter IV). And if spiritual well-being is to be fostered, what does this effort require?

First, Christian nurses themselves need to ask the Lord to empower them with professional competency and help them establish good interper-

---

[9] Shelly, J.A. and Miller, A.B. *Called to Care: A Christian theology of nursing*, Downers Grove: InterVarsity, 1999. 81ff.

sonal relationships. Nurses are expected to play multiple roles as consultants, comforters, and protectors of patients while managing their symptoms and employing their professional knowledge and skills; they are also expected to be physicians' working partners.[10] Christian nurses should be reliable partners for their colleagues.

By assuming the aforementioned roles, Christian nurses might be acknowledged as people who take their responsibility as providers of quality care seriously and who are cooperative team members. This reputation would naturally improve respect and trust in their relationships with colleagues. And so, patients and colleagues might be more willing to share their thoughts, feelings, and concerns about spiritual care. They might also be more inclined to regard Christian nurses as their friends in troubled times. Only then, with the patient's permission, should Christians share the Bible's teachings and their personal experiences regarding the meaning of life, suffering, and true comfort. Such opportunities for sharing can occur during daily nursing care routines, such as bathing or feeding patients. They can arise during quiet times when there are no immediate medical or nursing interventions required. Similarly, Christian nurses and their colleagues may agree to share personal and professional experiences regarding the meaning of life, suffering, and comfort which may lead to opportunities to discuss the Gospel message itself.

Finally, Christian nurses need to be aware that many patients' and colleagues' conceptions of health and illness and values and religious preferences are not derived from a Christian perspective but, rather, from new-age or other cultural perspectives. Christian nurses may carefully examine the philosophical backgrounds of their patients and colleagues and their understandings of care before providing spiritual care. Only by doing so will Christian nurses come to understand the cultural backgrounds of patients and colleagues and the implications of spiritual care in their daily nursing activities.[11]

---

[10] Shih 1995; Shih, F.J, and Chu, S.H. "Comparisons of American-Chinese and Taiwanese Patients' Perceptions of Dyspnea and Helpful Nursing Actions during the Intensive Care Unit Transition from Cardiac Surgery." *Heart & Lung* 28 (1999): 41-54; Shih, F.J. et al. "Turning Points of Surgical Cardiac Recovery during the Intensive Care Unit Transition." *Heart & Lung* 26 (1997): 99-108; Shih, F.J. et al. "Profile of the Ideal Nursing Image during the Discharge-Preparation Transition from Kidney Transplantation: Taiwanese Patients' Perspective." *Dialysis & Transplantation* 27 (1999): 269-288, 312; Shih, S.N, and Shih, F.J. "Health Needs of Elderly Chinese Men Living Alone with Heart Disease During their Hospitalization Transition." *Nursing Ethics* 6.2 (1999): 58-72.

[11] Shih 1996; Shih, F.J. et al. "Taiwanese Nurses' Appraisal of a Lecture on Spiritual Care for Patients in Critical Care Units." *Intensive & Critical Care Nursing* 15 (1999): 83-94.

4.2 Proselytizing by colleagues

Another dilemma that Christian nurses may expect is disagreement over sharing one's faith with the patient outside the context of spiritual care, i.e., situations in which colleagues are eager to share their religious affiliation, showing little respect for their patients' own attitudes towards that particular religious affiliation. So, with reference to the ethics of proselytizing as such (see Chapter IV), how are Christian nurses to act regarding a colleague in that kind of situation?

This kind of situation is, in fact, not uncommon in the daily practice of Christian nurses in the clinical setting. It may, however, be especially challenging for Christian nurses in developing countries where the Christian faith is not recognized, let alone the faith of a majority, so that Christian nurses are a minority group in their health care communities. Some nurses who have a faith other than Christianity, such as Buddhism, may encourage their patients to pray to Buddha for help in their condition. They may encourage belief in reincarnation or the afterlife, and encourage dying patients to practice religious rituals to prepare for the next life.

Again, the issue is that the well-being of patients is at stake. While Christian and nonchristian nurses may many times agree that a patient needs spiritual care, Christian nurses may feel that certain colleagues are threatening the patient's well-being rather than promoting it. They will then need to take a stand and speak up for the patient's benefit.

First, Christian nurses are advised to adopt a nonjudgmental attitude toward the person and foster good interpersonal relationships with their colleagues. With this positive approach, Christian nurses may then try to share their concerns about the issue with their colleagues, in private if possible (which may reduce the chance of the discussion being taken as negative criticism). In this way their colleagues may recognize that the Christian nurse has taken notice of the issue and is prepared to engage in a discussion where opinions are shared and patients' best interests are central. Colleagues may appreciate the Christian nurse's efforts to communicate openly.

Secondly, Christian nurses should be in touch with the leaders of their health care team. Sometimes they should call for a meeting, perhaps with formal records, for the purpose of formulating regulations to deal with disrespect regarding the patient's beliefs. Not only would the patients' human rights be protected if they did so, but discrepancies between health professionals (nurses with different religious affiliations in particular) might more easily be prevented. This clarification, in turn, could only be for the good of the patient, which after all is the professional responsibility of the nurse (see also Chapter V).

84

5. Alternative therapies

The fifth kind of dilemma that nurses frequently encounter relates to situations with colleagues involving alternative therapies (AT). This part of the chapter will focus on the nurse's responsibility in dealing with disagreements about AT within the team or profession; it will not discuss the acceptability of AT as such (see Chapter IX). The history of AT is a long one. In many societies the practice of AT was part of daily life long before the advent of Western medicine. Nowadays, a combination of Eastern medicine, often involving many AT, and Western medicine is not uncommon in various parts of the world. Although AT have been used for centuries, the theoretical rationale of many AT is still uncertain, or unknown, or insufficiently validated from the perspective of Western academic standards.

Three types of opinions held by health professionals in Western medical education regarding AT:

The first type involves the belief that the practice of AT is a nonscientific and second-rate type of medical regimen. This opinion is part of many health professionals' value system and has considerably contributed to their prejudice in regard to patient choice. The majority of health professionals in the Eastern and Western world hold this belief and would explicitly or implicitly tell their patients that the use of AT is inappropriate and that it would frustrate the outcome of treatment. In patients' minds, health professionals of this opinion are hostile to anything related to AT. The result is poor communication between patients and their health professionals about the practice of AT.

The second type of belief entails the assumption that the use of AT is good only for health maintenance or promotion while the person is not ill. In this situation, the health professional often asks patients to refrain from the use of AT during the course of their (Western) medical treatment. In patients' minds, health professionals of this opinion are more or less neutral in regard to use of AT. This position allows for some communication between patients and health professionals about the use of AT.

Third and last, there a growing conviction among health professionals that the use of some kinds of AT can enhance the effectiveness of Western medical regimes for certain diseases, in particular, chronic diseases. Health professionals who hold this view may or may not take the initiative to talk with patients about mixed treatment regimes involving both Western medicine and AT. Consequently, nurses are required to learn to practice different protocols and monitor patients' health status during mixed treatment.

A common dilemma in relation to this issue arises from the fact that opinions of different health team members about the value and legitimacy of AT differ from those of patients and their families (or significant others). Such differences may lead to particularly complex conflicts if the patient's health condition is very serious and his prospects bleak (as for instance, in the terminal phase of cancer). This disagreement may happen when patients and their significant others ask for the use of various AT and the physicians and nurses turn down their request. A special dilemma arises if patients and their families then turn to Christian nurses to ask for help in persuading other health professionals to allow them to try one or various kinds of AT. How should the Christian nurse deal with this kind of dilemma, given her professional responsibility (and assuming that she accepts at least some forms of AT)?

In such a case, it may not be the nurse's responsibility to decide whether or not AT are used; if the alternative is effective, treatment decisions are made by the physician and the patient. Nevertheless, the nurse will have a big role to play in the observation, information, and support of patients, even when she herself would refuse AT. Even more so, when she really thinks the patient's health or well-being is at risk here, she is to use her role to safeguard the patient's interests. How?

First, the Christian nurse may take the initiative and approach the health team members and the patient as well as his significant others to carefully clarify the various parties' beliefs and expectations regarding AT.

Secondly, if there are differences of opinion, the Christian nurse may seek to understand these and explore possible ways of resolving the conflict involving the patient, his family, and health team members.

Thirdly, the Christian nurse may suggest that the health team members consult experts on AT to clarify misconceptions about AT treatment proto-cols. The purpose should be to reach consensus on the practice of AT so that optimal benefits are obtained and any possible disadvantages or risks associated with the use of AT are minimized. The Christian nurse may ask the leader of the health team—in most cases, the physician—to call a meeting to clarify the related concerns.

Lastly, the Christian nurse may invite patients and their families to par-ticipate in discussions on this issue with their primary physicians in the pres-ence of all health team members. In this case, the nurse may act as a liaison between patients and the health team. The nurse often spends more time with patients and their families and hence can be more familiar with the patient's communication style and patterns of expression. Thus, the nurse may help relieve patients' uneasiness communicating with people of author-ity such as physicians. Hopefully, with the nurse's help, the patient and his relatives and other health professionals may engage in fruitful discourse, clarifying their concerns, so that differences may be resolved and conflicts avoided.

6. Misconduct by colleagues

The last kind of dilemma that nurses, and in particular Christian nurses, may expect in relationship to colleagues arises if they find that a colleague is violating policy or breaking the law. An example would be stealing medical supplies or medication, perhaps even from patients (which constitutes abusing the patient as well). This phenomenon is not uncommon in health delivery systems where storage and use of medical supplies or medication are not closely monitored.[12]

On reflection, there are different types of problems in this area. Of course there is misconduct in the sense of patient abuse. Here, colleagues have a professional responsibility to protect the patient. In other cases, such as stealing supplies or covering up errors, the patient's well-being may not be directly affected. But even when it doesn't seem to hurt anyone, nurses are to uphold certain standards of professional conduct, including promoting trustworthiness and dependability. For Christian nurses, such standards may conform to the biblical commandments against theft and dishonesty. Having made this point, the nurse must also be practical. Here are some recommendations for Christian nurses about how to handle such situations.

First, the Christian nurse may take the opportunity to inform the particular colleague that she has noticed his or her behavior and that it was not appropriate. If possible, the nurse should urge the colleague to put things back. She may try to convince the colleague of the inappropriateness of his or her behavior.

Secondly, the Christian nurse should ask the ward manager to improve the safety and efficiency of the process and outcome of diagnostic and treatment, including recording and accounting for materials and medication used.

Thirdly, the Christian nurse may take steps to care for the colleague and try to help him or her follow the new policy related to the use of materials and medication whenever possible.

Finally, the Christian nurse should talk to the ward manager privately and ask for help in clarifying her role in dealing with this issue. Christian nurses may act on the basis of biblical guidelines and bear witness to Christian virtues in dialogue between nurses acting inappropriately and ward managers or other administrators. The Christian nurse may further ask the

---

[12] Take only the evidence for this in the annual reports of the UKCC on professional conduct.

87

ward manager to call periodical meetings to discuss actual and related ethical problems. Health care providers may then be given opportunities to address problems encountered, the context of problems, choices, and feasible strategies for managing problems in a Christian way. The decisions or suggestions of the meeting should be formally recorded, dispersed, practiced, and periodically evaluated.

7. Conclusion

The effects of globalization are influencing health care increasingly and not least in regard to health care values. However, globalization does not necessarily mean that the world becomes one global village; there will also be fragmentation and distortion of local communities. Rather, it means that Christian nurses in the 21st century have the challenge and the opportunity to reach out worldwide and help one another to live as members of the body of Christ in their profession.[13] Having the privilege of being a nurse, the question is "How can I repay the Lord for all his goodness to me" (Psalm 116:12)? The answer would be to show the richness of the Lord's goodness through good care for others. But in the complex and demanding world of nursing care in this century, Christian and nonbelieving nurses alike are wise to be aware of their own beliefs and values in order to recognize the requirements of total patient care, and particularly of its ethical dimension.[14]

Concerns about ethical issues call for constant dialogue with others nurtured and inspired by God's word and the Holy Spirit. A good relationship is a firm bridge. With the help of this bridge many goods from the Lord and humankind can be shared in a triangular way–between the Lord, others, and oneself. If this bridge is damaged or broken, the communication of these blessings is frustrated and the door to those blessings might be closed. Therefore, a good relationship between nurses and their superiors and colleagues has become more important than ever. Although it is sometimes difficult to foster long-term and trustworthy relationships in today's societies, with faith Christian nurses should ask the Lord to grant them and their

---

[13] Cusveller, B. and Shelly, J.A. *Christ, Culture and Christian Scholarship in Nursing: Report of an academic conference*. http://www.gospelcom.net/iv/ncf/facgrad/600scotland.htm (Sept. 1, 2000).

[14] Ashworth, P. "Spiritual Care: A challenge in multicultural critical care." *Intensive and Critical Care Nursing* 15.1 (1999): 63-64; Shih, F.J. et al. 1999, 83-94.

(possibly nonbelieving) colleagues good relationships, built on the foundation of a compassionate and just mind. While an active prayer life may not in itself be a professional responsibility for Christian nurses, prayer may come as a direct consequence for Christian nurses.

Christian nurses should ask the Lord to give them opportunities to learn to establish good relationships with others in meeting the various ethical challenges in our professional tasks. Nevertheless, let us remind ourselves that not all challenges in the interaction between Christian nurses and their colleagues regarding their professional tasks necessarily amount to disagreements or dilemmas. Rather, these challenges are related to the interaction between the multifaceted backgrounds that frame the value systems and personalities of every individual nurse and his or her colleagues. Whether in our personal or in our professional life, these value systems and personality structures guide the process and determine the outcomes of choices when faced with ethical dilemmas both in daily life and in critical moments—today and in the future.

Nurses are like an angel's brightest eyes in both the patient's darkest night as in their colleagues' darkest night. In addition to patients, colleagues who are suffering may also be helped spiritually through a Christian nurse's warm hands. A nurse's quality of care is like a heavenly cradle for his or her patients and colleagues in pain, no matter what is in their heart or body. The conceptual and moral schemes that frame good nursing are also the soul of true care. Meanwhile, good interpersonal relationships between nurses, their colleagues, and their patients can serve as a vessel for blessings from the Lord. Quality of professional interpersonal relationships is a result of give-and-take, of the dynamic and uncertain processes of complex interpersonal relationships. For professional nurses to win this land for the Lord they must walk closely with the Lord in faith, spending quiet times with the Lord, reading God's word, and praying for God's guidance and protection whenever and wherever needed. Whoever is willing to hold these keys has the promise of victory in the never failing name of Jesus Christ.

Some verses from Scripture to encourage reflection on the character of the Christian nurse when facing ethical challenges:

"So I turned my mind to understand, to investigate and to search out wisdom and the scheme of things" (Ecclesiastes 7:25).

"Give to Caesar what is Caesar's and to God what is God's" (Mark 12:17).

"The most important [commandment]," answered Jesus, "is this: Hear, O Israel, the Lord our God, the Lord is one. Love the Lord your God with all your heart and with all your soul and with all your mind and with all your strength. The second is this: 'Love your neighbor as yourself.' There is no commandment greater than these" (Mark 12:29-31).

"Let us consider how we may spur one another on toward love and good deeds" (Hebrews 10:24).

"He is not the God of the dead, but of the living ..." (Mark 12:27).

"'What do you want me to do for you?' Jesus asked him. The blind man said, 'Rabbi, I want to see.' 'Go,' said Jesus, 'your faith has healed you.' Immediately he received his sight and followed Jesus along the road" (Mark 10:51-52).

"By faith Abraham, when called to go to a place he would later receive as his inheritance, obeyed and went, even through he did not know where he was going" (Hebrews 11:8).

"Jesus looked at them and said, 'With man this is impossible, but not with God; all things are possible with God'" (Mark 10:27).

"So do not throw away your confidence; it will be richly rewarded. You need to preserve so that when you have done the will of God, you will receive what he has promised" (Hebrews 10:35).

"He will be our guide ..." (Psalm 48:14).

Discussion questions

1. Some situations test a nurse's commitment to work with other nurses in order to achieve high-quality care for patients. What would your response be to nurses who fail to uphold professional standards or who break the law?

2. Given a nurse's professional responsibility, how much attention should they pay to a patient's relatives or significant others?

3. How should nurses work with colleagues who hesitate to provide spiritual care for a patient with spiritual needs?

4. How should a nurse respond to disagreement about alternative therapies within the team or profession?

5. What would you say to the three nurses in the opening vignette? What are your arguments for or against a strike?

7

Professional Responsibility in Interdisciplinary Health Care Teams and Cooperative Working Relationships

Jan van der Wolf

Vignette

Mr. Vanden Berg underwent surgery for an intestinal tumor. Today, he is quite restless and anxious. Repeatedly, he asks Martine, his nurse, what his prognosis is. She is aware of the prognosis–actually quite bleak–but it is the responsibility of the attending physician to discuss that with him. The physician had already agreed to have this conversation, but until now hadn't had a chance. Martine feels bad about the fact that she repeatedly has had to refer Mr. Vanden Berg to the physician. At the end of the day, the patient is literally panicking. Martine calls the physician and informs him of the situation, but he indicates that he sees little opportunity to talk to the patient before the next morning. Out of respect for Mr. Vanden Berg's situation, she really considers it irresponsible to wait until the next morning. She experiences the whole situation as a huge dilemma.

1. Cooperation: a professional responsibility

1.1 Introduction

Nurses work together with physicians and other employees in health care institutions. Together they try to serve the patients' interests. Their cooperative working relations, however, also generate areas of tension, including ethical conflict. How do dilemmas such as the one in the above vignette materialize? And what are nurses to do about them? To help nurses answer these questions, several other questions are first put forward and answered in this chapter:

- What is the professional responsibility of nurses in cooperative working relations? (Section 1)
- What factors influence those cooperative working relations? (Section 2)
- Which moral problems can be expected to occur in cooperative working relations? (Section 3)
- How can nurses deal with these from a Christian perspective? (Section 4)

In this chapter, the focus is on individual nurses rather than on the profession as a whole. We will examine certain work-related factors, particularly those affecting teamwork. This chapter limits itself to one clinical context, namely the hospital. Consequently, cooperation in certain other fields of nursing is given scant attention. The emphasis, furthermore, is on the primary task of nurses: direct patient care. Yet, it could be argued that the nature of cooperation between nurses and (in particular) physicians in one clinical context is also applicable to other health professions and clinical fields.

1.2 Nursing's practical responsibility and cooperation

Nurses have their own professional, that is, practical responsibility for patient care. They also have a professional responsibility to support other professionals involved in patient care (see Chapter II). They are to carry out their own responsibilities while cooperating with others to serve the health interests of patients. Yet, in some situations, their own primary responsibility clashes with their responsibility to cooperate with others. This dilemma raises the question of how nurses ought to cooperate with others when such conflicts arise. In other words, how is the nurse's primary responsibility related to the responsibilities of other professions in health care? For an answer, we must look at the position of the nurse in relationship to others in cooperative working relations.[1]

The position of nurses in working relationships with others has traditionally been represented in three ways:[2]

- In the "military model," the nature and structure of the relationship was determined by "unquestioning obedience." Nurses would act as subordinates or handmaidens of the doctors.
- The "legal model" was introduced in response to the emergence of the emancipated patient in the 60s and 70s. This perspective aimed at advancing the autonomy and the rights of patients. Nurses became negotiators and advocates of patient interests (see Chapter V). Sometimes this interplay resulted in conflicting stands vis-à-vis physicians.
- The "market model," the third model developed, involves the application of business administration to care practices. This mentality resulted in the efficient use of resources becoming a predominant value. Physicians and nurses are now reduced to providing institutional services to patient consumers.

The third model has not supplanted the first two. Each of the three accentuates a different aspect of the nursing position. Each model puts forward an aspect still to be found in the present practice of care. Physicians, patients, and institutions continue to exercise their influence on the work of nurses. Together, they constitute the field in which nurses are to exercise their responsibility. The responsibility of the nurse, to put it differently, is "squeezed" between the demands that are put forward by

- the authority of medical personnel,
- the interests of patients,
- the regulations and management of the institution. [3]

Seen in this way, nurses can be characterized as "people in between."[4] This position can be visualized as follows on the next page:

---

[1] Holm, S. *Ethical Problems in Clinical Practice. The ethical reasoning of health care professionals.* Manchester: Manchester University, 1997; Chambliss, D.F. *Beyond Caring: Hospitals, nurses, and the social organization of ethics.* Chicago: University of Chicago, 1996.

[2] Oak, J.C. "A Conflict of Loyalties: Nursing, conscientious objection, and JCAHO HR.5." *Making the Rounds (in Health, Faith, and Ethics)* 1.12 (1996): 1, 3-5, 8.

[3] Cf. Tschudin, V. *Ethics in Nursing.* Oxford: Butterworth-Heinemann, 1992². 103-124. See also in Benjamin, M. and Curtis, J. *Ethics in Nursing.* New York: Oxford University, 1992³ Ch. 4 and 6.

[4] Bishop, A.H. and Scudder, J.D. *The Practical, Moral and Personal Sense of Nursing.* Albany: SUNY, 1990. 20.

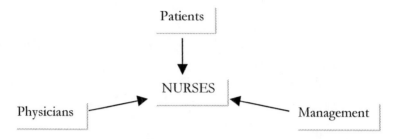

Figure 1. Nurses between other actors in health care.

This "in-between" situation has traditionally been regarded as beset with problems and as having negative effects on cooperative endeavors. Many point towards differences in status and power, thereby frustrating nursing practice. Of course, we must not close our eyes to factors that would impede cooperation, such as the misuse of power, unwillingness to cooperate, and poor communication. But there are also reasons to view this "in between" situation positively. Could it not give nurses a strategic position and even a certain freedom in the exercise of their responsibilities? We assume at this point that nurses understand the medical perspective, that they know the policies and procedures of the institution, and that they, as a rule, have close relationships with patients. In this kind of situation, nurses have unique opportunities—not available to other caregivers—to carry out their responsibilities of care in the service of the patient's health interests. In this position, they serve a unique "bridging function" between patients, physicians, and institutions, which can be illustrated as follows:

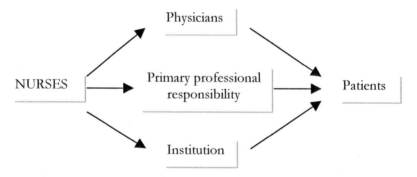

Figure 2. Nurses have their own direct responsibility towards patients (care, support, advocacy). In carrying out certain responsibilities, nurses are dependent on the cooperation of physicians (for instance, medication) or of the institution (for instance, the availability of nursing supplies).

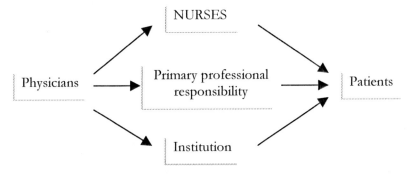

Figure 3. Physicians have their own direct responsibility towards patients (examination, treatment). For certain responsibilities, they need the cooperation of nurses (for instance, administering medication) or of the institution (for instance, facilities for examination and treatment).

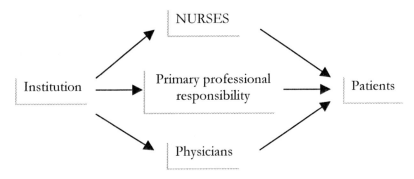

Figure 4. Institutions have their own direct responsibilities regarding patients (for instance, facilities). For certain responsibilities, they need the cooperation of the nurse (monitoring patients) and of physicians (for instance, hospital admission and discharge).

On this line of thought, we discern that nurses have two core responsibilities. Besides their primary responsibility, the provision of care, they also have a responsibility to support other professionals. This responsibility is also central to their practice. In particular, they help physicians and institutions fulfill their responsibilities. This support is not part of their nursing care but involves a coordination of their care with that of others. In this view, nurses' professional responsibility becomes a means of proactively utilizing their position in this quadrangle of relationships rather than seeing it as a nasty problem. It follows that patient care is not necessarily served by a stricter delineation of which practices fall within the boundaries of each profession. Such efforts can become forced attempts to close gaps in the fence around the boundary of each profession. Well-known are discussions

95

between physicians and nurses about the degree to which a given patient should undergo further diagnostics or therapy, or whether the patient should be allowed to rest. The mutually shared goal of care is not always best served by squabbling over such "border incidents."

1.3 Cooperation: between authority and autonomy

We can now state our basic starting points regarding cooperation between nurses and other health care professionals (physicians, in particular):

- There is a primary responsibility for each professional practice,
- There is an equal footing of disciplines,
- There is shared responsibility, and
- Reciprocal support is a professional responsibility.

A short description follows of these points. Chapter II already posited certain starting points in the professional responsibilities of nursing and medicine. We recall that medical care focuses on treatment of the patient's illness and handicap: to remove or prevent the disruption of his ability to exercise the fundamental functions vital for human life. Alongside this medical responsibility, nursing care focuses on the effects that illness, handicap, and medical care have on the patient's ability to exercise fundamental functions vital for his life as a human being. Neither type of care is reducible to the other, nor are they mutually exclusive.

Because of the specific professional responsibilities as well as the shared responsibilities, both professional practices are to be regarded as having an equal standing and as being mutually dependent. The Christian perspective on responsibility, largely implicit here, offers us some "control beliefs"[5] that help us steer away from two common misconceptions. The one is that nurses are subjected to physicians' authority on a merely hierarchical basis. One's professional responsibility is to support others in as far as the patient's condition requires this ("functional" authority; cf. Chapter V). The Christian way to say this is that nurses are to *serve* physicians—and physicians are to serve nurses—in as far as this service serves the patient. The other misconception is that nurses and physicians are both autonomous health care professionals, negotiating the other's contribution to a patient's own care. This idea denies that nurses and physicians (and other health care professionals) share a common goal, i.e., the interests of the patient. In short, nurses and physicians serve the patient together, albeit each in their own way.

---

[5] The expression "control beliefs" originates in Wolterstorff, N.P. *Reason Within the Bounds of Religion.* Grand Rapids: Eerdmans, 1984; cf. Bouma H. et al. *Christian Faith, Health, and Medical Practice.* Grand Rapids: Eerdmans, 1989. 28.

The central purpose or value of both care practices is the advancement of the health and welfare of the patient "as intrinsically valuable."[6] Considering this common focus, members of the nursing and medical professions should not seek conflict but recognize that they have a common responsibility to engage in consultation and cooperation in order to promote their basic end. Each profession requires the support of the other in order to support the patients. Cooperation is part of the core responsibility of both professions. Given the nature of professional nursing practice and present developments in care, what is at issue is central to all professional care practices. It is part of the responsibility of health care professions to fulfill their shared responsibility to promote effective·care for patients by means of optimal cooperation.

The four starting points discussed above provide a Christian framework for the way nurses notice, understand, and address ethical tensions regarding cooperation. Whether or not cooperation–and thereby overall patient care–is based on these starting points depends on several factors. When those involved do not have the opportunity to cooperate as required by these starting points, certain moral problems arise. In the following section we will address these kinds of situations.

2. Cooperation: structural, cultural, and personal factors

Many different aspects naturally influence the quality of cooperation. Foremost, in our opinion, are the views held by practitioners concerning their professional practice and their corresponding roles. This factor is in addition, of course, to the attitudes and skills of the persons engaged in cooperation. Other powerful influences on cooperation are to be found in certain characteristics of organizations, including policy making, information dispersal, frequency of team meetings, decision-making procedures, pace of decision making, and mutual and intercollegial support.

Before we address certain ethical bottlenecks facing cooperation, we must first probe the factors causing these bottlenecks. Regarding cooperation, nurses have task-oriented responsibilities, people-oriented responsibilities, and the individual responsibility to keep a balance between those two. Among the factors influencing the quality of cooperation (and there may be more), we can distinguish between structural, cultural, and personal factors.

---

[6] For this expression see Puolimatka, T. *Moral Realism and Justification*. Helsinki: Finnish Academy of Science and Letters, 1989. 144; cf. Hoogland, J. and Jochemsen, H. "Professional Autonomy and the Normative Structure of Medical Practice.' *Theoretical Medicine and Bioethics* 21.5 (2000): 457-475.

2.1 Structural factors

Cooperation between professionals can be affected by the structure of an organization and by the professional's own position and role-descriptions. Important factors are the structural form of the organization, its communication lines, committees, team meetings, decision-making procedures, professional codes, and protocols. Health care institutions are characterized by having many different professionals closely interact. This is in contrast to many other modern institutions, for instance, schools, where we find only one type of professional, that is, the teacher. In health care, the aim of realizing good care is shared by different groups of professionals, which makes the provision of care a complex matter. Mutual, careful, and prudent behavior, involving a high degree of cooperation between groups of professionals, must be the standard here.

2.2 Cultural factors

Besides structural factors, we also find cultural factors influencing cooperation. These are implicit codes for interpersonal conduct, intercollegiate relations, working climate, attitudes, habits, intentions, and institutional treatment and health care philosophies. The culture of an institution, or a department, can be said to be the sum total of views, patterns of conduct, and beliefs that personnel share with each other. Understood in this way, the culture encompasses rules for conduct and reciprocal expectations within the organization. At issue is not the number of meetings held, but the manner and the atmosphere of those meetings, whether people are vulnerable, whether certain topics can or cannot be discussed, and whether the meetings are highly formal or not.

Caregivers' often nonverbal frames of reference influence their conduct. These may or may not provide health workers with the opportunity to attach importance to matters transcending their own person such as a shared philosophy of care and common goals. In some institutional cultures, we find uncertainty about the rules for organizational behavior resulting in minimal awareness of shared expectations. In such situations there will be no understanding of how to conduct oneself vis-à-vis others in cooperative ventures.

2.3 Personal factors

A good institutional structure and positive culture do not, however, necessarily entail good cooperation. A third factor is crucial: the manner in which cooperating people conduct themselves. Briefly stated, personal characteristics of cooperating practitioners do play a role. These characteristics may be communicative, social and relational skills, the ability to engage in dialogue with the use of arguments, personal values and norms, beliefs and views concerning one's own and others' professions, the manner of handling one's (professional) responsibility, and the ability to relate to and accept others. For successful decision-making, much can depend on familiarity and mutual appreciation. Moreover, it makes a difference whether nurses are sufficiently skilled in reasoning, verbalizing, and disseminating beliefs concerning professional knowledge, professional standards, goals, and moral judgments. Besides these skills, positive attitudes and motivation are also necessary. The quality of cooperation is advanced considerably if nurses can personally share the same values, norms, and aims in their practice.

3. Moral problems in cooperative relations

Exercising professional responsibility while engaged in cooperative relationships is a complex matter given the diverse (structural, cultural, and personal) factors just mentioned. When those factors are not properly tuned into each other, certain problems arise. Here, we will focus mainly on moral problems.

Cooperative problems need not necessarily be moral problems (disagreement about a budget might not be a moral issue), and moral problems need not necessarily be cooperative problems (disrespectful behavior towards another person is not necessarily a cooperative issue). At the same time, in practice, moral problems are often strongly interwoven with cooperative problems.[7] Therefore, it may often be difficult to discern the moral issues at stake. Conversely, moral issues relating to cooperation often cannot be solved in a detached manner without paying attention to their context. This requirement is certainly true in the case of moral problems caused by cooperation and due to the complexity of different structural, cultural, and personal factors.

To gain a proper understanding of these matters the following questions are raised and addressed in this section:
- When do nurses experience problems as moral problems?
- When can we speak of a moral problem in cooperation?
- Which moral problems can be discerned in cooperative situations?
- Which points need special attention by nurses?

---

[7] Cf. Holm 1997, Chambliss 1996.

3.1 When do nurses experience problems as moral problems?

As a rule, nurses appear to experience problems as moral problems in two situations:

- when the patient is caused harm or injury;
- when the nurse feels powerless to change an undesirable situation.[8]

In the first case, given their attachment to the health interests of the patient, nurses experience a moral problem when, in their view, patients or their families could be harmed. In this situation they may see a contrast between what ought to be and what is, which in situations of cooperation may mean that an "intermediate position" cannot be adopted and that it is difficult, or even impossible, to challenge decisions that are detrimental to the welfare of the patient.

Secondly, nurses may experience a problem as moral when they experience lack of power and influence and feel that they can do nothing about a problem. They see a contrast between what ought to be and what can be done. Such a feeling of powerlessness is usually caused by factors that nurses feel to be beyond their ability to change. There are two sides to this matter. First, there are factors that *factually* lie outside their direct sphere of influence (for instance, inadequate working conditions or factors such as appointments being made without consultation). Secondly, feelings of powerlessness may be caused by their own self-image and *belief* that they have little influence, irrespective of whether this belief is correct or not. This conception complies with the negative approach to the intermediate position of nurses. And it may involve the belief that nurses have a lower status than doctors and so have little influence on policy making, in particular concerning immediate patient care. It may involve a belief that nurses have an unequal standing in relationship to other professions, or enjoy little respect and appreciation from other professions (whereas, in truth, this may not be the case at all!).

3.2 When can we speak of a moral problem in cooperation?

Moral problems in cooperation arise when:

- nurses cannot act or engage in cooperation as they should in view of their professional responsibility, or
- nurses are urged to act or cooperate in ways that are not in keeping with their professional responsibility.

These situations are characterized by frustration in achieving the central moral good of professional nursing practice, namely the advancement of patients' health and welfare. Achievement of this moral good is thwarted,

---

[8] Arend, A.J.G. van der, and Remmers-Van den Hurk, C.H.M. "Moral Problems Among Dutch Nurses: A survey." *Nursing Ethics* 6.6 (1999): 468-482.

thus creating a moral conflict. Perhaps the situation involves another value not necessarily within the realm of the professional nursing responsibility, such as confidentiality concerning the private lives of physicians or, perhaps, involving nonmoral interests such as the feasibility of a schedule. The core of these moral conflicts consists of a clash between nursing standards, conduct, and responsibility, on the one hand, and the responsibility and interventions of others, for instance, physicians, managers, and administrators. A problem of cooperation can, but does not have to, grow into a full-fledged moral conflict. Whether it does depends on the degree to which nurses have insight into the causes of the problem and are in a position to discuss them.

In this situation, it is imperative to distinguish between two questions which suggest two approaches to resolution:

- Who is accountable to whom about what (orientation on professional responsibility)?
- By which structural, cultural, or personal factors is the problem influenced (orientation on circumstances)?

The limitations ultimately faced by nurses in the performance of their moral responsibility are therefore not simply the fault of other professionals. Problems may also be caused by limited organizational, cultural, and personal possibilities. Sometimes apparently a dilemma relates to the very perception of professional responsibility and entails, for instance, a lack of knowledge about its scope, resulting in inappropriate role expectations. In this event, wrong concepts should be tackled and there is no question of personal or relational faults. Under the right conditions, nurses, too, can revise their ideas and views while negotiating with physicians or while participating in the decision-making process of a multi-disciplinary team. Thereby choices may be made which comply with nurses' expectations.

Of course, it can happen that nurses and physicians persistently differ in their judgment of "what is best for the patient." Approaching the question from different professional perspectives involving different responsibilities, they may adopt stands which exclude consensus. This is not necessarily always a problem of cooperation. The degree to which nurses can respectfully accept disagreement is determined by the respect afforded them in earlier negotiations and discussions.

3.3 Which moral problems can be discerned in cooperative situations?

Factors that may lead to moral problems in cooperation may–as has been explained–be grouped together as structural, cultural, and personal factors.

To start with, let us focus on how organizational structure and organizational culture allow professionals to make decisions and implement these when dealing with morally sensitive issues. Problems may arise when the nursing responsibility and the responsibilities nurses share with others are insufficiently supported by the structure (for instance, due to lack of consultative situations) or culture (for instance, negative and complaining attitudes). It matters whether the raising of sensitive issues is viewed positively or negatively. Does the exercise of professional and institutional responsibility regarding problems in existing consultative situations stimulate the moral climate or frustrate it? The provision of care involves being held accountable for (moral) choices. Decisions are to be justified, amongst other things, by prudent and careful weighing of the different viewpoints. Responsible cooperation calls, in short, for consultative structures that serve the professional responsibility of each profession, and the mutual coordination of the same, as well as shared responsibilities.

In addition to structural and cultural factors, the attitudes and behaviors of individual nurses also play a role here. To what extent are nurses willing and able to make moral choices and exercise responsibilities in cooperation with others? It need not be a question of whether the nurse is properly motivated or professionally competent. The demeanor of nurses when cooperating with others may be influenced by other personal factors such as age, view of life, personal norms and values, gender, experience, education, proficiency, skills, social-communicative skills, motivation, personal or emotional attachments, and views about the profession and about responsibility. Moreover, personal and organizational factors usually interact. We can illustrate this by mentioning: inadequate self-images of nurses and inadequate exercise of skills by nurses.

In the first case, nurses sometimes may adopt a submissive role because of feelings of powerlessness. Experiencing a lack of influence on or compared to other professions, they may place themselves in the position of the underdog. This sense of inferiority may result in behavior that demonstrates apathy, noncommunication, avoidance, and denial. Such behavior may have varied causes. Previous attempts to blow the whistle on moral problems may have led to disappointing results. Furthermore, a number of factors can influence "moral inaction" (which may, of course, be a deliberate choice). Among these are a superficial insight into nursing practice, lack of relevant moral motivation (in particular in relationship to other professions), poor ability to relate to others (the greater the ability to relate, the greater the assertiveness), a failure to recognize what one's own values and norms are, and faulty views on what professional responsibility requires.

102

A second personal source of moral problems is the absence of relevant skills. Sometimes nurses *think* that they are not qualified to challenge other professionals (the problem of inadequate self image). And sometimes nurses are *actually* incapable of proper social communication and argumentation ("I can't explain what I feel"). These shortcomings inhibit nurses' attempts to address moral problems, negotiate with physicians, and so forth. Joint decisions and solutions then become difficult to realize. In such cases, nurses may just become inactive or silent and not share their anxieties. In addition, these kinds of factors frustrate the exercise of moral responsibility in teamwork.

3.4 Which points need special attention by nurses?

It has been suggested that problems of cooperation do not have to be caused by ill-mannered physicians or brainless managers. Indeed, problems can originate from a combination of factors, including the way nurses view themselves and their ability and opportunity to cooperate. We will now turn to some specific obstacles experienced by nurses in their dealings with other health care professionals.

Personal, cultural, and structural factors influence the manner in which cooperating professionals carry out their moral responsibility. This issue does not primarily relate to the question of whether morally appropriate choices are made while cooperating. Rather it concerns the question of whether the teamwork itself meets certain moral standards (besides the choices being made). There are two ways of achieving morally adequate teamwork:

- The first has to do with the willingness and competence of practitioners to realize their own moral responsibility.
- The second way is the manner in which moral issues relating to the teamwork of both professions can be addressed and the degree to which the arrangements and nature of dialogues make this possible or difficult.

The quality of the teamwork is mainly evidenced in the willingness to engage in dialogue and then how that dialogue is conducted. Lack of dialogue and poor dialogue are two of the obstacles leading to moral dilemmas for nurses.

A significant obstacle experienced by nurses is the type of situation where they are not allowed to make decisions themselves (consider the case study at the beginning of the chapter). Nurses may confront moral problems when decisions are made under the jurisdiction of the medical profession or the management. They may still be faced with the consequences of

such decisions made by others and ensuing dilemmas. These may complicate their work or generate all types of consequences (e.g. a failure to know
how to answer questions and comments by members of the patient's family). How nurses handle these problems may depend on various conditions
such as time pressures, the degree to which nurses experience the situation
as an invasion of their own professional responsibility, the degree to which
they do or do not participate in activities with which they disagree, their
moral sensitivity.

These situations may be caused by, among other things, a lack of information, lack of consultations, and poor involvement in decision-making
regarding ethically significant issues. Lack of information concerning ethical
decision-making may come about not only because nurses do not participate in decision-making, but also as a result of deficient communication.
Relevant information may, for example, not be found in the patient's records, in which case it may be impossible to trace the grounds for a certain
decision. Even if there has been a joint decision, the grounds for the same
may be unclear.

The extent to which nurses may participate in ethical decision-making
depends, among other things, on the manner in which multi-disciplinary
consultations are organized on various levels and the way they work. Thus it
may depend on whether the staff-meetings are multi-disciplinary, or on
whether moral quandaries are explored in multi-disciplinary dialogue. According to a Dutch survey, compared with other health care sectors, the
hospital environment is the least open to dialogue about ethical issues in
consultations involving head-nurses and physicians.[9] The findings might be
different in other countries, such as the U.S. where all hospitals are required
to have ethics committees that are multidisciplinary–not just doctors and
nurses, but pharmacy, chaplaincy, administration, residents, and a lay community member. Quite possibly this requirement is due to the central role of
medical staff in this clinical setting. There, the deliberation by the medical
staff is the locus for addressing ethical issues. Top management in hospitals
seems to ask advice more often from medical staff than from middle management. The participation of the "shop floor" in discussions of ethical
problems (which ought to be noticeable in middle-management consultations) is the lowest in hospitals.

---

[9] Willigenburg, T. van, et al. *Ethiek, levensbeschouwing en het management.* Utrecht: Nationaal
Ziekenhuis Instituut, 1991. 68 ['Ethics, Religion, and Management,' Dutch Hospital
Federation].

4. Ends and means: personal, cultural, and structural

We have pointed to several factors and obstacles that may bring about (moral) problems in teamwork relationships between nurses and others. The nurses' professional responsibility cannot be divorced from structural, cultural, and personal factors in their actual workplace. Given these factors and obstacles, we will close this paper by addressing the possibilities and means nurses have to exercise their moral responsibility while engaged in cooperative ventures.

- To address this issue we will deal first with the competence and skills of nurses.
- Secondly, we will argue that increased participation by nurses in ethical decision-making calls for changes in many existing practices found in the structure and the culture of organizations.
- Thirdly, it is important to learn how to respond to opportunities for moral decision-making in particular situations.

Our focal point will be the vignette with which this chapter commenced. What can Nurse Martine do to solve her dilemma?

4.1. Personal contribution and competence

What do nurses need to improve teamwork? Could it be a strong sense of their own moral values, normative beliefs, or professional responsibility? Could it be a certain view of mutual responsibilities based on the imperative to carefully conduct oneself morally? Or could it be the recognition of and respect for the independence and uniqueness of each professional practice? Or would it be the ability to fulfill personal, relational, and functional aspects of cooperation? Or would it be knowledge of the role of culture and organization of the institution? Or could it be knowledge of the possibilities and consequences of the nursing profession's involvement in teamwork? Without a doubt, *all* of these factors count since care is very much a "team sport" and the professional skills of the nurse must include communication and reasoning on moral matters. Lack of power does not always have to be attributed to the position or the personality of nurses. The ability of nurses openly to criticize certain kinds of behavior on the part of physicians can be improved by training and improvement of nurses' skills. In addition, the following personal qualities call for special consideration: (1) motivation or moral courage, and (2) sensitivity or compassion.

First, *motivation* and *moral courage* matter. We are not assuming that nurses lack good attitudes. But through "resocialization"–an understandable way of adjusting to existing subcultures–nurses' willingness to criticize the moral quality of certain practices may diminish. The less open the climate is on the ward, the less watchful nurses may choose to be. The ability to engage in careful and prudent moral discussion while cooperating with others requires personal courage to raise issues. This need for bravery is particularly true if one runs the risk of becoming unpopular. Also, it requires courage to refuse superficial solutions and to reject participation in endeavors contrary to patients' interests such as disrespectful behavior, which is contrary to nurses' professional responsibility.

The use of protocols or professional practices based on professional codes may easily be marred by a lack of motivation and courage. "Whistle blowing," or drawing attention to faults and immoral behavior of colleagues, is a good illustration of this lack (Chapter VI). It strikes at the core of existing loyalty between professionals. The consequences for relationships and teamwork are often wide-ranging. Yet, when nurses remain silent and postpone discussion of wrong practices, the patient's interests will be compromised.

According to nurses' codes, action is required or appropriate in the following kinds of situations:

- when the nurse discovers behavior of colleagues or other professionals detrimental to the patient's interest. Here the nurse takes measures to protect the patient.
- when the nurse *acts* to safeguard the patients and the public and when health care and safety are affected by the incompetent, unethical, or illegal practice of any person.[10]

Secondly, *moral sensitivity* or, better still, *compassion* is important (cf. Chapter III). Despite the need for improved skills, professional conduct, and codes, nursing care must not become devoid of a feeling of solidarity with the suffering human. This virtue, with a Christian connotation, goes beyond mushy emotions and does not limit itself to subjective "feelings." It allows one to empathize with the other and to actually do what one would like to have done to oneself. Moreover, compassion for patients strengthens one's moral sensitivity and emphasizes the moral dimension of care. It provides an antidote to a single-minded legalistic use of ethical codes, professional rules, and protocols. We must avoid using formal regulations for self-justification (such as resorting to excuses such as "this is not my responsibility") rather than for the purpose of improving the moral quality of our professional conduct.

---

[10] American Nurses Association. *Code for Nurses with Interpretative Statements.* Kansas City: ANA, 1985 (italics added).

4.2 Culture: "strategic" functioning as nurses' responsibility

The improvement of cooperation is not a matter of incidental and clever solutions. Even if nurses personally are quite competent, often there is something within the culture of a department or an institution that must be changed in order for professionals to work together properly. Traditional positions, differing professional views, and the like make it difficult to put moral questions concerning existing cooperative culture in the foreground. Whoever aims for a "quick fix" may easily become disappointed. "It takes too much time," is a well-known bias (one that also contains a value judgment). Creating an open moral climate takes time, resolve, and effort.

Besides time and determination, there is also the need to think of alternative approaches. We are faced with the challenge of finding a way between the desire to address all types of deficiencies in cooperation immediately and, on the other hand, an attitude of "What do I care?" This challenge calls for a certain degree of strategy, in other words, a purposeful and gradual effort to improve matters. It is important to start a process of generating (or designing) organizational and cultural conditions for change. The emphasis here should be on working from the bottom upwards, promoting situational factors that contribute towards increased nursing participation in ethical decision-making. Such a strategy asks for systematic, long-term thinking transcending the daily care practice.

Such strategic thinking and conduct promoting enhanced ethical consideration entails the following requirements:

First, there must be reflection on the practice and quality of cooperation. What are the weaknesses, what are the barriers, and which contributing factors can be recognized? Are these relational or communicative in nature; are they influenced by (sub-)cultural and institutional organization? Alternatively, what role is played by factors such as competence and differences in nursing philosophies or professional views? Whether the weaknesses are of the former or the second kind makes a considerable difference to the way problems are handled.

Secondly, it is important to make sure matters are handled feasibly; establishing goals, thinking in time periods, acting systematically, and accepting the need for long-term planning, which entails being proactive, even while experiencing psychological resistance or when there appears to be minimal support for engagement in moral deliberation. However, if one can convince colleagues of the feasibility of gradual change, their approval may more easily be gained. In this respect, an important objective could be to regularly put certain issues on the agenda, getting interested colleagues more involved, or actively pursuing the need for policy instead of ad-hoc solutions.

Thirdly, in addition to weaknesses and barriers, in every cooperative venture there are also opportunities for change. Thus it is wise to avail of existing practices or policies. Availing of existing openings for contribution and participation calls for a creative, perhaps, unconventional approach. In a situation like the Dutch one, the large number of laws aimed at improving the position of patients and residents provide ample opportunities for improving structural cooperation through, for instance, consultation and reporting. Increasingly, new developments in organizations call for less responsibility dictated from above, resulting in, for example, self-governing teams. The increasingly frequent calls for quality provide another opportunity for change. Here it may be a matter of pointing out the consequences of, amongst other things, the philosophy of nursing care, or the identity of the institution. Patient satisfaction with care provided is increasingly dependent on more than one profession. It is the result of, for example, multidisciplinary cooperation and reciprocal sensitivity to other professions.

4.3 Structure: possibilities for ethical consultations

Coordinating care (giving shape to one's own professional responsibility and, especially, dealing with the range of responsibilities of various professionals) requires fruitful dialogue. The interests of patients do not allow extemporization or inconsequential decision-making. Why should future cooperation not be improved, given the changes in the relationships between many professions in today's health care?

To succeed in this regard we must look beyond personal competencies and institutional culture. Certain structures are also necessary. Particularly important is the establishment of opportunities for organized moral consultation. The general context must be reckoned with here. Situations in which it is necessary to make fast decisions and act quickly (for instance, in the case of resuscitation) are not amenable to this. Situations involving moral incidents and questions are often better evaluated in retrospect (for instance, "Did we have to go on for so long?").

To respond better in future situations, one needs to come to agreement with others, calling for consultations. In general, each health care situation, each department has its own particular recurring situations that are morally sensitive and cause problems and dilemmas for nurses. These patterns make it possible to anticipate difficult situations. It is part of the departmental responsibility to create structural designs for consultation and promote existing openings for negotiation. This method holds for long-term planning

108

as well as for the periodic manner in which agreement is realized in practice. Such issues as failure to keep promises and working agreements must also be addressed if only to avoid misunderstanding and undermining desired cooperation.

In nurse-physician cooperation there are two kinds of situations in which ethical care consultations are especially called for.

- The first is when nurses signal an undesirable development, as when the medical policy agreed to is unclear.
- The second kind of situation is when the physician has taken a (tentative) decision that has adverse repercussions on the nurse.

Physicians discuss treatment with patients, including the moral implications of the same. That practice means that physicians, literally speaking, do not have to justify their instructions to nurses. However, in regard to ethically sensitive decisions, this choice can easily lead to resentment and misunderstandings. To comply with such a decision, nurses should at least be given the opportunity to understand "why" the particular decision in question has been made so that they can understand why it is acceptable and even necessary.

Regarding the reporting of problems and the justification of decisions, often the dialogue between physicians and nurses needs much improvement. A possible means of encouraging teamwork in this respect is, for instance, the publication of a list of problems recorded by nurses in advance of interdisciplinary moral deliberations. Another possibility is the establishment of regular dialogues. It is wise to use existing patterns of dialogue (team meetings, multidisciplinary negotiations, nursing councils) for this purpose. It is also wise to be as specific as possible in making suggestions and proposals because many of the matters debated in ethical consultations are considered vague and redundant–and often end the dialogue. In achieving effective ethical decision-making, the identification of moral alternatives and clear and concise reports of decisions should be reported in accessible documents.

5. Conclusion

Nurse Martine, introduced at the beginning of this chapter, experienced a moral problem while consulting the physician about the patient, Mr. Vanden Berg. As we have seen, she may follow several paths. Regarding the immediate need of the patient, she may choose an "emergency option." In this case she either informs the patient herself, or she applies pressure to the physician to do so. She will then be required to justify her decision in retrospect by reference to her conviction that she acted in the best interests of the patient. Whether this kind of conduct would harm the existing team-work depends on structural, cultural, and personal factors, in particular vis-à-vis the physician.

Finally, Martine is advised to discuss this dilemma with her head nurse or senior staff members so that agreements may be made regarding similar situations in the future. However, she also ought to gain a better under-standing of the various factors at the root of the dilemma she faced, includ-ing factors relating to herself. This knowledge will allow her to anticipate similar difficulties in the future.

Acknowledgement

The author wishes to thank Mrs. Sonya Grypma of Lethbridge, Canada, and colleague Johan Hegeman of Ede, The Netherlands, for their valuable feedback on an earlier draft of this chapter.

Discussion questions

1. There is strong emphasis in this chapter on the nurses' own professional responsibility in cooperative relationships. Do you agree with the four ba-sic starting points in section 1.3 (primary responsibility for each profes-sional practice, equal footing of disciplines, shared responsibility, reciprocal support)?

2. Which factors most affect your own contribution to patient care in multid-isciplinary teams (see section 2)?

3. After reading this chapter, this question remains: which immediate course of action do you think Nurse Martine could and should take in the situa-tion of Mr. Vanden Berg (see vignette)?

4. Which factors caused her moral dilemma?

5. Which strategic influence could and should Martine try to exert afterwards on the cultural and structural level?

110

8 .

Professional Responsibility at the End of Life

Euthanasia and palliative care

Ada van Bruchem-Van de Scheur

Vignette

Two years ago, Mrs. Hansen, 58, discovered a lump in her breast. After medical examination, breast-cancer was diagnosed. A removal of the breast followed, with removal of axillary glands, where some metastases had been found. After a strenuous course of chemotherapy that appeared to be successful, her condition deteriorated very quickly again, much to everyone's disappointment. What could still be done for her?

1. Introduction

The unique role of nurses includes "helping people … in the performance of those activities contributing to … a peaceful death," says Virginia Henderson in her well-known definition of nurses' professional responsibilities.[1] The growing numbers of elderly people in most Western countries and the increasing acceptance of euthanasia in some of them make it im-

---

[1] Henderson, V. and Nite, G. *Principles and Practice of Nursing.* New York: Macmillan, 1978[6].

perative that the contents and limits of this responsibility be clarified. In view of the many cases of euthanasia reported in Dutch surveys (2700 in 1990, 3500 in 1995, and 3800 in 2001) and the numbers actually reported to the Dutch authorities (486 in 1990, 1466 in 1995, and 2054 in 2001),[2] it is clear that nurses will be increasingly involved in this thorny area of health care.

This chapter addresses nurses' responsibilities at the end of life and some accompanying ethical dilemmas, especially as they pertain to euthanasia and conscientious objections. In this chapter we will consider

- the growing importance of palliative care and a nurse's professional responsibility in this area of care (section 1.1);
- the question of what is to be counted as euthanasia (section 2);
- the contents and limits of nurses' professional responsibility when confronted with a request for euthanasia (section 3);
- the question of how to handle one's conscientious objection to euthanasia (section 4).

1.1 Palliative care

Within the practice of health care, it is not unusual to distinguish between preventive, curative, and palliative care:

- Preventive care aims at avoiding potential health problems,
- Curative care aims at remedying actual health problems,
- Palliative care aims at health problems that cannot be (wholly) prevented or cured (anymore), but the symptoms of which can still be relieved.

The last may benefit patients with certain chronic conditions (such as Parkinson's disease or arthritis). In most cases, however, it involves care for patients with terminal conditions, especially cancer. The remainder of this chapter deals primarily with the latter kind of situation.

Nursing care for the terminally ill has developed a distinctive profile in recent years. Palliative medicine has improved considerably over the past few decades. Many of the health problems that accompany terminal illnesses, such as pain, nausea, and fatigue, can be treated in much better ways than was the case some time ago. The development of better pain medication has been important, as has the development of holistic palliative care, comprising treatment, counseling, pastoral care, and support for the family, all within one health care setting.

This holistic approach to palliative terminal care is above all the fruit of the hospice movement, whose foundations were laid in England around

---

[2] Keown, J. and Jochemsen, H. "Voluntary Euthanasia under Control? Further empirical evidence from the Netherlands." *Journal of Medical Ethics* 25.1 (1999): 16-21. Wal, G. van der, et al. "Medische besluitvorming aan het einde van het leven. [Medical decision-making at the end of life]" Utrecht: De Tijdstroom, 2003.

1900. The early hospice institutions received more widespread attention when Cicely Saunders started to practice and articulate the ethos of modern hospice care. In response to threats to human dignity which arise within aspects of modern health care, she founded St. Christopher's Hospice in London and so initiated the now global hospice movement.[3]

The fundamental inspiration for Saunders' life work was her Christian faith. The development of the hospice movement is not so much dependent on existing facilities as on the communication of a specific philosophy of care.[4] This philosophy rests on the following principles:

- Patients with incurable conditions are not beyond all medical treatment or unworthy of any medical attention. Rather, holistic care is indicated for patients' physical, mental, social, and spiritual needs. Medical attention will not be directed to the cause of the illness but to its injurious side effects, so that dying will be accompanied by as little suffering as possible.
- Treatment aimed at either unnatural prolongation or unnatural shortening of patients' lives is to be withheld.
- A multidisciplinary team (for instance including an oncologist, nurses, an anesthetist, a psychologist, a pastor, and volunteers) is to be available.
- Awareness of death and dying is to be promoted. The hospice movement values a change in the mentality and attitude of society towards dying, and encourages the view that death is a part of human life.

Palliative care includes a moral attitude and commitment towards good care for terminally ill patients (and their spouses, families, and friends!). It involves, in other words, a professional responsibility to give patients the care they need to die as peacefully as possible. The value of the lives of patients underlies this approach. In the euthanasia debate, palliative care is sometimes presented as an alternative to euthanasia. Christian institutions which reject euthanasia sometimes develop policies that attempt to eliminate the situations which lead to requests for euthanasia. They are to be commended for this effort! In fact, the practice of adequate palliative care seems to minimize the number of requests for euthanasia. However, we should not forget that palliative care is valuable in itself as good care for terminally ill patients.

1.2 Nurses' responsibilities in palliative care: an overview

What are nurses supposed to do when caring for terminally ill patients? In palliative care, the meaning of dying for patients and relatives occupies a central place. To illustrate this reality, we will follow the fourfold distinction

---

[3] Janssens, R. *Palliative Care: Concepts and ethics.* Nijmegen: Nijmegen University, 2001. 38-47.
[4] Bradshaw, A. "The Spiritual Dimension of Hospice: The secularization of an ideal." *Social Science and Medicine* 43 (1996): 409-419.

commonly used in nursing, namely, between physical, mental, social, and spiritual aspects.

Physically, effective pain control is central to optimal care. Pain is usually experienced as the most exhausting and distressing complaint. Anxiety and fatigue may further intensify the experience of pain, thus calling for holistic treatment. In many cases pain can be relieved; in other cases it can at least be made more bearable. Besides pain, insomnia, restlessness, nausea, itching, diarrhea, and constipation are complaints calling for attention. Each treatment requires a careful assessment of its appropriateness, involving the weighing of its burdens and benefits.

In addition to the need for competent physical care, terminally ill patients have many *mental* needs, calling for human compassion and attention. This response does not necessarily imply long conversations. The mere provision of competent care may very well express nurses' commitment to the well-being of patients. A keen eye for what is bothering patients and their relatives is of fundamental importance, especially when patients are experiencing loneliness, pain, shortness of breath, or fear of these things. The very fear of possible suffering may paralyze patients. What is called for on the part of nurses is sympathy; they must let patients express their fears and troubles, and they must look for what can be alleviated or remedied. Last but not least, nurses need to give patients the assurance that they will not turn their back on them when in desperation but will stay close whenever that is necessary.

From a *social* point of view, patients often prefer to live out their last days in the intimacy of their own home, surrounded by the people with whom they have shared good and bad times. Wherever patients stay, their loved ones are their most important companions. Nurses may step in to complement those companions. Patients and their loved ones may be too upset emotionally to cope with the situation. They may say, "It was so good together" or "I wanted to see the children grow up." Sometimes it is difficult for patients because they are self-employed, in which case it may be useful to help them make contacts for their financial arrangements or getting their will in order. Given the social nature of patients' well-being, it is also important that nurses reach out to their families and friends. There are several reasons for doing so:

- The next of kin experience their difficulties coping with problems, such as being left behind.
- Support for the next of kin enables them to maintain better relationships with patients.
- Care given to the next of kin also models how they can care for patients, enabling them to maximally participate in patients' care.

114

Friends and relatives, then, also need care and to play a role in the provision of care. Nurses' professional responsibilities for the terminally ill, therefore, also involve care of the (future) bereaved.

Lastly, the *spiritual* aspects of palliative care must be recognized. "It always happened to someone else, but I never thought about my own death. Why me? Why now? What's the point?" These are the sorts of questions one often hears in the crisis precipitated by being terminally ill. Most often, questions of meaning are central. People question the meaning of life, the meaning of being ill, the meaning of dying, and so on. Spirituality arises outside religious contexts and applies to more than religious convictions. It also involves asking such questions of meaning.

When one listens carefully, one may detect feelings of hopelessness and helplessness. An attentive attitude is of great importance in the face of spiritual suffering since this may enhance nurses' understanding of patients' worldviews. To talk about such matters presupposes finesse, authenticity, and closeness on the part of nurses. An open-ended question may be indicated to help patients verbalize their spiritual needs. "How do you look back on your own life?" or "How do you see the future?" are examples. These questions need to be expressions of compassion for a fellow human being as well, lest they do more harm than good. The fundamental attitude of nurses must be one of respect for the religion or worldview of patients, without denying or imposing their own (cf. Chapter IV).

2. Types of decisions at the end of life

Caring for terminally ill patients sometimes brings nurses face to face with ethical issues. Being faced with patients who express a wish to have their life ended is one of those. To clearly see what is at issue, we need to consider different types of decisions about the care and treatment of dying patients. They will be illustrated against the background of the Dutch euthanasia practice, the present author being Dutch, as this context will help to clarify the discussion. Using case histories, we begin by discussing types of decisions that may lead to a patient's death but which should not be called euthanasia. These are

- withholding a medically futile treatment,
- refusal of treatment or care by patients,
- optimal treatment of pain, and
- withholding futile nourishment.

Secondly, we will discuss types of measures that *are* properly called euthanasia (and assisted suicide):

- termination of a patient's life without their own request
- termination of a patient's life on their own request
- physician-assisted suicide.

2.1 Decision-making in good terminal care

In this section, we refer to the vignette in the opening paragraph of this chapter.

> Mrs. Hansen turned out to have numerous metastases in the bones and a resulting severe anemia. The intervals between the required blood transfusions rapidly became shorter. At a certain point the physician suggested stopping this increasingly burdensome procedure even if its continuation might be able to prolong Mrs. Hansen's life. She herself also recognized the futility of the treatment and agreed.

This situation involves the cessation of treatment that has become medically futile because the burden of the treatment outweighed its benefits for that patient's condition. Even if the patient's life would be prolonged to some extent by continuing the blood transfusions, we do not call discontinuing them (either indirect or direct) "euthanasia." The intention behind stopping the treatment is to spare this patient further burdensome treatment with no recognizable benefits; the reason is not to shorten the patient's life (although this may be a foreseeable, yet unintended consequence). Stopping treatment in this situation is ethically justified. So is withholding treatment:

> Mrs. Hansen's physician did consider the possibility of another transfusion. He knew, however, that Mrs. Hansen had indicated that she did not want to start any more treatments in such a situation. She would certainly have refused burdensome measures even if they would have prolonged her life a little longer.

The death of patients following their refusal of further treatment is also not a case of euthanasia. Patients have a right to respect their personal and physical integrity. In many countries, this right is incorporated in health law, stating the legal right of patients not to be subjected to medical treatment unless they have explicitly given their permission for it (informed consent). If terminally ill patients do not accept the side effects or other drawbacks of some medical regimen and, hence, die sooner than would otherwise have been the case, other things being equal, it would be justifiable to respect their choice from a medical-ethical point of view. Of course, there may be other points of view that may make patients choose differently (for instance a Christian's different view of autonomy), but it would not be against good medical practice.

> After a week, Mrs. Hansen is admitted to the hospital because of severe pain. There she is administered morphine intravenously. The pain medication is slowly increased whenever she reports increasing pain.

In this situation, the treatment of the suffering patient may have the side effect of shortening the patient's life. The primary intention of the palliative

116

measures, however, is to alleviate suffering in the last phase of the patient's life. Eventually, she will die of her terminal condition, not of the palliative measures. Hence, the possible effects on the process of dying are ethically acceptable because they are linked to the palliation necessary for the condition of the patient.[5]

> After a few days, Mrs. Hansen has weakened to the extent that she refuses to eat and drink. Her body does not seem to accept any more nourishment or hydration. She is sleepy and often nauseated. The nurses only attend to her oral hygiene.

There has been much debate concerning the appropriateness of dehydration in the case of dying patients, i.e., withholding food and fluids.[6] One of the central points in these debates is whether feeding and hydration (even if artificial) should be considered medical treatment. If not, there may be no medical grounds for such withholding, as fluids and nutrition are basic human needs. Yet, on the basis of "quality of life" considerations, it is sometimes decided to stop feeding a terminally ill patient and so, effectively, to bring about his death.

However, terminal dehydration can only be ethically justified under either of two conditions. These are when

- the body of the patient does not seem to accept nourishment anymore (which may happen when the moment of death is close), or if artificial feeding causes mostly further pain.
- the patient consciously refuses to accept any more nourishment. Here, respect for patients in the terminal stage of their dying process, tired of life and of suffering, means that one does not force-feed them and so accepts their decision.

In all other cases, the caring team has a responsibility to provide optimal patient care, including offering nourishment, and withholding it amounts to intentional termination of life.

2.2 Forms of euthanasia

A second group of decisions comes at the end of the patient's life.

> Meanwhile, Mrs. Hansen has become comatose and her children have been with her for two days. Yet, she does not die, wherefore her family urges the physician to give her "a last push" because, so they say, this is a meaningless situation. What's the use laying there like that? The physician

---

[5] Keown, J. "'Double Effect' and Palliative Care: A legal and ethical outline." *Ethics & Medicine* 15.2 (1999): 53-54.

[6] Craig, G. "Palliative Care from the Perspective of a Consultant Geriatrician: The dangers of withholding hydration." *Ethics & Medicine* 15.1 (1999): 15-19; De Ridder, D. and Gastmans, C. "Dehydration among Terminally Ill Patients: An integrated ethical and practical approach for caregivers." *Nursing Ethics* 3.4 (1996): 305-316.

decides to increase the dose of pain medication and orders the nurse to administer the drug. The nurse questions the ethics of this measure and is hesitant to increase the morphine dosage. Mrs. Hansen, after all, appears to be comfortable and free of pain.

Would this decision constitute euthanasia? This would be a case of euthanasia if more medication were administered than was necessary for adequate pain control and given with the intention of causing the patient's death. The point is that the goal of good palliative care would then be replaced by another goal, namely that of shortening, or terminating, the patient's life. The physician's decision regarding Mrs. Hansen would then involve euthanasia without the patient's request, or nonvoluntary euthanasia.

In the Netherlands, however, this case would not involve euthanasia in the strict sense of the definition in use, which requires the patient's voluntary request. Mrs. Hansen's case would be termed "termination of life without request." The defining conditions of euthanasia in the strict sense are as follows:

- The act is performed with the intention that it should result in the patient's death,
- It involves the administration of a drug by a physician, following
- A voluntary and well-considered request from the patient.[7]

Euthanasia in this strict sense has been legalized in the Netherlands, not euthanasia in the nonvoluntary sense.[8]

Let us consider another example:

Mr. Young suffers from cancer of the prostate which has metastasized. His condition is deteriorating daily and his death seems only a matter of weeks away. His wish is to die at home, in the presence of his wife and children. He takes morphine for the pain. This occasionally makes him sleepy, which forces him to stay in bed for most of the day. He has always abhorred this kind of dependence on others. Consequently, he sends his written request for euthanasia to his family doctor (a "euthanasia will"). On his own, Mr. Young decides to take less pain medication so that his mind is clearer when his doctor arrives, two days later.

---

[7] Arend, A.J.G. van der. "An Ethical Perspective on Euthanasia and Assisted Suicide in the Netherlands from a Nursing Point of View." *Nursing Ethics* 5.4 (1998): 307-318: "In accordance with official Dutch terminology, euthanasia is defined as intentionally ending the life of a person, upon his or her explicit request with the act being performed by someone other than the person concerned"; Muller, M.T. et al. "The Role of the Nurse in Active Euthanasia and Physician-Assisted Suicide." *Journal of Advanced Nursing* 26 (1997): 424-430: "euthanasia is the intentional termination of life, by someone other than the patient, at the patient's request...."

[8] But see Keown and Jochemsen 1999.

After Mr. Young discusses his request for euthanasia with his family doctor, they agree to proceed. As this illustration is drawn from the Dutch context, another doctor is consulted in accordance with the procedures required by law in the Netherlands for the practice of euthanasia.[9] At the agreed time, the family doctor returns to the house, talks to the next of kin, and asks Mr. Young if he persists in his request. He does. The doctor administers an injection containing a sedative, followed by injection of the lethal drug. Mr. Young dies in the way he had asked to.

Here we find a different case of life-terminating intervention to that of Mrs. Hansen, namely euthanasia in the voluntary sense.

If it had been possible, Mr. Young would have preferred to take the lethal drug himself, for instance in the form of something to drink. This would have allowed him to show that it was truly his own personal wish to die. But because he complained of severe nausea and had problems swallowing, another course of action was needed.

Consuming the lethal overdose oneself would be called "physician-assisted suicide." From a practical point of view, a physician performs euthanasia, but the patient himself performs suicide by taking drugs provided by the physician. From an ethical point of view, this is a life-terminating act that does not differ significantly from euthanasia in the voluntary sense. From a legal point of view, the two types of actions are treated differently both in The Netherlands and in the state of Oregon in the United States. The professional responsibility of nurses, however, would be the same. Both ethically and legally, nurses may never (help to) administer the lethal dosage.[10] Recall our definition of nurses' professional responsibility was that it is to foster patients' health and well-being by attending to the effects the patients' health disorders have on their capacities to live their daily lives as human beings (see Chapter II). Nowhere in this responsibility does the need to end patients' lives arise. Quite to the contrary!

3. Nurses' professional responsibility when confronted with a request for euthanasia

In care surrounding a patient requesting euthanasia, it is not unusual to distinguish four phases: observation, decision making, performance, and aftercare (for the relatives).[11]

---

[9] Jochemsen, H. "Update: The legalization of euthanasia in The Netherlands." *Ethics & Medicine* 17.1 (2001): 9-10.

[10] Compare a discussion of the Dutch situation in Daverschot, M. and Wal, H. van der. "The Position of Nurses in the New Dutch Euthanasia Bill: A report of legal and political developments." *Ethics & Medicine* 17.2 (2001): 85-92.

[11] Scheur, A. van de, and Arend, A. van der. "The Role of Nurses in Euthanasia: A Dutch study." *Nursing Ethics* 5.6 (1998): 497-508.

In care with direct relation to measures aimed at the termination of life, nurses' professional responsibility mainly pertains to the first two of these four phases; responsibility also pertains importantly to the last phase. We have seen that nurses have no professional responsibility to execute euthanasia although they are often present when it occurs.[12] Nevertheless, when confronted with a request for euthanasia, nurses remain responsible for providing the best possible care for patients in the other three phases of their practice. It is of the utmost importance, therefore, that Christian nurses do not withdraw too quickly from caring for patients who ask for euthanasia by appealing to their conscientious objection to euthanasia. In doing so they would fail to fulfill their professional responsibilities during the last phases of patients' lives, precisely when those responsibilities ought to be fulfilled. We will now turn to nurses' professional responsibilities for patients who have requested euthanasia.

3.1 Observation of a request for euthanasia

> Mr. De Vries suffers from an inoperable cancer of the pancreas. Because of extreme pain caused by metastases on the peritoneum, he is admitted to the hospital. When his nurse Else helps him to wash himself in the morning, he confides to her that he sees no more sense in going on. Some months earlier he had signed a "euthanasia will" and now feels it is time to die.

Often, a request for euthanasia is initially addressed to nurses, for instance during physical care. It will not always be immediately evident what patients mean by such a request. Patients may even formulate their request differently with nurses than with physicians, perhaps because nurses are not allowed to perform euthanasia and so would respond differently. In some cases, patients just want to air their feelings or ask for compassion or company. It is noteworthy, however, that patients themselves have started to use the term "euthanasia" more openly than before.

Even when patients really mean to express a wish to die when requesting euthanasia, exactly what they plan to do may differ from patient to patient. Patients may have different periods of time in mind, for instance. Some patients might speak of "now" or the "present" without meaning today. Some would really mean *today* and expect things to be realized within the hour. Other patients would have some moment in the foreseeable future in mind, sometimes even the exact place and time. Still others may speak of a general "future" and mean some time when their condition has deteriorated:

---

[12] Van de Scheur and Van der Arend 1998, 499, 502-503.

"If such-and-such happens, then I don't want to live any longer." Such a request is sometimes made after being confronted with bad news about their condition.

Notwithstanding the differences among individual patients and between their requests, the following guidelines may help nurses caring for patients who ask for euthanasia.

(1) When patients initially request euthanasia, it is of prime importance that nurses *listen* carefully. Nurses should not immediately start thinking about possible responses or about ways to prevent euthanasia, or about the best way to express objections to the request. Rather, listening requires really trying to understand what a patient is saying. Patients direct their wishes to nurses because they want to be understood, even if their wishes are provocative. And nurses show understanding by really listening to what patients are saying, not by thinking about what they themselves would say. For nurses to show that they are trying to understand patients is not the same as agreeing with them.

(2) In conversation with patients, nurses should seek to find out whether they've interpreted requests for euthanasia adequately. The following three steps can assist here:

- Nurses should check whether they have correctly understood what the patient has actually said. They may do so by rephrasing the patient's request in their own words: "So by saying … you mean …" and the like.

- Nurses should check if there is some hidden request for help behind the request for euthanasia. In order to ascertain whether this is the case, they may take into account the four aspects of the model of palliative care used in section 2.

  - The physical aspect: pain, ulcerated tumors, shortness of breath, incontinence of urine and feces, constipation;
  - The mental aspect: fear of the unknown, depression, confusion;
  - The social aspect: loneliness, quarrelling;
  - The spiritual aspect: loss of meaning, bitterness.

  Analyzing a request for euthanasia in light of these four aspects of palliative care provides a structure for choosing between possible palliative care options.

- Nurses should check if the request actually originates with the patients themselves. Relatives or others may have influenced the patient's feelings about terminating his or her life. This persuasion may happen, for instance, when relatives are no longer able to cope with the situation.

121

(3) Nurses should explain that they are not the ones to be approached with a request for euthanasia, if only because they can never administer the lethal drugs. It is up to patients to address a physician with such a request.

(4) Finally, nurses should inform patients about their own views regarding euthanasia (but see section 4.2).

(5) Nurses should discuss with patients whether others, for instance relatives or fellow nurses, might be informed about the request for euthanasia. Such information should only be given with the patient's permission. Likewise, if patients address their request for euthanasia to the physician first, the physician should not inform the nurses about this unless the patient has given his or her permission. If patients make a plea for secrecy or confidentiality, this should be respected. Consequently, if a patient's request to the physicians was confidential, no nurses will be involved in the process. In practice, this kind of secrecy is more frequent in home care or community care situations than in hospital or nursing home situations where physicians and nurses work together more closely.

3.2 The decision-making phase

The aim of clinical decisions in this context is to proceed in a well-considered manner and adopt a responsible approach to patients in the terminal stage of their disease, an approach based on an analysis of the request. When nurses are caring for a patient who has asked for euthanasia, it is clear that optimal care will require their participation when deciding on the right course of action. Given their daily involvement in patients' situations, they may have much to contribute to the physician's careful choice of options. Whether or not the physician decides to grant a patient his or her request for euthanasia remains solely the physician's own responsibility (albeit, according to us, not his *professional* responsibility).

However, nurses and physicians have a professional responsibility to jointly provide optimal care for patients. Therefore, nurses ought to be consulted. They contribute to the analysis of the request and the assessment of the different options of palliative intervention. Nurses and physicians (and others) make complementary contributions to the discussion of patients' requests (Chapter VII).

Although nurses have an important professional role to play in all the choices pertaining to patient care, many Christian nurses may not agree. If they act on this assumption, however, information about a patient's condition which they have gathered while providing patient care and their knowledge about his or her request will not be taken into consideration in future planning of care. As a result, suggestions they may have about how to improve the patient's care will not be heard. Nurses may sometimes feel intimidated in these situations and therefore not accept that they have a professional role to play. They may think that nurses with conscientious objections should withdraw completely from caring for such patients. But surely this is an unwarranted limitation of their professional responsibility and at the same time excludes people with certain convictions regarding euthanasia.

To be sure, Christian nurses' participation in the decision-making process does not guarantee that euthanasia will be prevented. Well-considered discussions of a request for euthanasia may not even lead to a consensus. When a physician decides to grant a patient his or her request for euthanasia, there is no professional responsibility for nurses as far as the execution of euthanasia is concerned (but of course, their responsibility for all other aspects of care remains). What the decision entails, perhaps, is a moral obligation to express objections to the physician and a legal responsibility to notify the head nurse, hospital management, professional organization, or even the authorities. Sometimes an ethics committee or hospital chaplain can help by acting as negotiators here. Of course, in extreme cases, that kind of action may cause trouble for Christian nurses and lead to a deterioration of the working environment in the wards. We would not be prepared to claim that they always have a responsibility to push matters to these extremes. Sometimes it is wiser to accept certain decisions in order to make other important gains in relationships with patients, the physician, or others.

4. Nurses, euthanasia, and conscientious objections

4.1 Objections

When nurses are confronted with requests for euthanasia and refuse to take part in such an action, they may appeal to any of the following three kinds of objections:

- A professional objection,
- A legal objection, and
- A principled objection (or conscientious objection).

Before we say anything about these kinds of objection, we must ask *to what* precisely nurses may object. Naturally, nurses cannot object to the whole care of a terminally ill patient, even if this patient has asked for euthanasia. After all, providing care is the core of their professional responsibility. Therefore, their responsibility to observe patients and make decisions that promote optimal care remains. Nurses are correctly expected, then, to provide patients care with respect and dedication, irrespective of their moral judgment of euthanasia.

Nurses may object to (participation in) any intervention directed against the life of patients. As we said, nurses do not have a professional responsibility for the execution of euthanasia as far as cooperation with a

123

physician is involved, let alone for an intervention that is directed against the central value of nursing care (which is fostering the capacities of a human being to live well). The first objection, in short, is that participation in the proficient execution of euthanasia is not a part of nurses' professional responsibility because it runs counter to the principles of their profession (as laid down in professional codes and declarations).

Secondly, euthanasia remains illegal in most countries. These laws apply to physicians as well as nurses. In most countries not only is euthanasia a criminal act, but so too is aiding and abetting its performance (such as assisting a physician by providing means, opportunity, or information leading to the successful act of euthanasia). Nurses who refrain from involvement in euthanasia, therefore, remain on solid legal ground in most parts of the world.

Thirdly, in addition to these two objections, nurses may rightfully object to euthanasia on principle. For instance, they may have moral or religious convictions prohibiting them from granting euthanasia. It is generally accepted in most countries that conscientious objections ought to be respected, for instance in countries where abortion is a legal possibility. This right is definitely valid in the case of euthanasia.

When nurses have decided about what exactly they object to and where their remaining responsibilities lie, they have to find a way of exercising these responsibilities in practice. Let us conclude this chapter by focusing on the question of how nurses, despite having conscientious objections to euthanasia, may continue to carry out their responsibilities, particularly in relation to patients, colleagues, and the institution or health care facility.

4.2 In relation to patients

When nurses have adequately understood a patient's request for euthanasia, it is generally desirable that they inform the patient of their own stand on the matter. In some countries, professional guidelines even declare this personal revelation to be a professional duty.[13] This duty (if it is a duty), however, cannot be isolated from the professional responsibility to provide optimal care for dying patients. Therefore, when the condition of patients does not allow discussing moral points of view, it may be morally responsible to refrain from doing so. But if mutual ignorance would not be beneficial for a good nursing relationship, then it is, indeed, part of nurses' professional responsibility to inform patients, as illustrated in the following case.

> *Else*: I appreciate that you confide in me and express your wish to die, but I do not concur with your request for euthanasia.

---

[13] In the Netherlands, for instance, the joint professional guidelines of the medical association KNMG, and the nurses' union NU'91.

De Vries: But why do you object to euthanasia?

Else: It is my conviction that I have a professional responsibility to provide optimal care, rather than inflict harm. In the end, life is a precious gift from God.

De Vries: Yeah right, some gift when your life is like this. That's easy for you to say, when you're up and walking around as you are. You know, what you believe is your business, but I don't buy it.

Else: I've told you my point of view because I believe you ought to know what your nurse is thinking. You know as well as I do, that opinions on euthanasia differ these days.

De Vries: Sure, you have a right to speak for yourself. But this is my decision, which I have made a long time ago. You shouldn't let it upset you.

Else: It isn't my intention to let this difference of opinion influence our relationship in a negative way. On the contrary, if you feel like talking about it with me, please feel free at all times.

A recent survey among Dutch nurses shows that nurses do not always inform patients of their own point of view, mainly because they find this conversation difficult.[14] Sometimes, the most important reason inhibiting them is their previous, and often negative, experiences with patients such as when they were not successful in "getting across" to patients or they experienced a loss of trust. Nonconfrontational behavior, however, will often result in an ongoing inward struggle while caring for the patient, a struggle that may even persist after the patient's death. The organized character of euthanasia may reinforce this struggle, especially when the last opportunity to point patients to the way of faith is inescapably getting closer. To avoid this kind of complication of the nursing relationship, nurses had better be open. It is certainly not our view that they should relieve their conscience or try to convert patients at any cost. It is their professional responsibility to speak about those things in a way that is beneficial for the nursing relationship, i.e., for providing optimal total patient care for the terminally ill.

4.3 In relation to colleagues

When planning patient care nurses should discuss each other's norms and values in terminal care. It is important that nurses know one another's ethical positions regarding patient care. This knowledge benefits cooperation in the team. Thus, training in discussion techniques will be helpful here as well as in basic patient care. Nurses often seem to categorize each other silently, yet they may find they agree more when they speak from the heart. When a team of nurses is divided into two camps, proponents and opponents of euthanasia, there is little to gain. Their professional responsibility may even be frustrated by such disagreement.

---

[14] Van de Scheur and Van der Arend 1998, 504.

Following patients' request to terminate their lives, a few days usually pass before the euthanasia actually occurs. In principle, objecting nurses may provide any care necessary for the patient's terminal condition (except for terminating his or her condition). Strictly speaking, nurses do not need to be present when the lethal drugs are actually administered because that is up to the physician. It is also not the responsibility of nurses to ensure that they are replaced from that shift. After all, this type of intervention should not take place at all. In practice, however, it is often agreed that a nurse who is going to be present when the patient dies will also undertake the required care in the last stages of the patient's life.

4.4 *In relation to the institution*

Dilemmas in direct patient care should also be addressed by institutional policies. An important question is whether a health care facility has a policy for conscientious objections. The theory that everyone is entitled to make conscientious objections does not always correspond to actual practice. The consequences of conscientious objections range from being ignored to being fired–not to mention the fact that applicants may be turned down in selection procedures. In some countries, health care institutions have put their euthanasia policy in writing. It is important to be aware of such policy statements. They may contain guidelines and restrictions, as well as rules about how to appeal to higher authorities within institutions when needed. Once institutions have openly accepted euthanasia, as in the Netherlands, nurses cannot strongly influence policy. But wherever the policy provides openings to influence actual practice–on the ward, in the ethics committee, wherever–nurses do have a professional responsibility to seize any opportunities and plead for the best possible care for dying patients.

Discussion questions

1. What is the difference between euthanasia and other decisions regarding the end of life?

2. How would you respond to a request for euthanasia? What is your professional responsibility toward the patient when a request occurs?

3. Do you think there is a connection between good palliative care and the prevention of euthanasia?

4. Sometimes a decision has to be made about whether or not to stop treatment. What would be your contribution as a Christian nurse in a team meeting regarding such a decision? What knowledge, skills, and attitudes would you need?

5. Suppose the decision has been made to stop treatment of a patient you know well. Furthermore, suppose that your conscience is really bothered by this decision. What would you do?

126

9

Professional Responsibility Concerning Alternative Therapies

Dónal O'Mathúna

Vignette

Lori, a Christian home care nurse, drove up to Mrs. Murphy's house along a twisted gravel road. Lori thought Mrs. Murphy looked brighter than usual as she greeted her at the door. "How was your vacation, Lori?"

"It was great! Very relaxing. But how have you been?"

"Oh, not too bad, I guess. The other nurse, Jackie, who came out while you were away was very nice. She would sit and chat, like we do. Still, it wasn't the same as when you visit me."

"I missed you too. But, tell me ... how has your arthritis been?"

"Well, pretty good. But, you know what?" Mrs. Murphy added excitedly. "Jackie did something I've never had before. I'm surprised you never told me about it. She called it 'ray-key,' or something like that. It certainly did the trick for me on one bad day. Do you know what it is?"

"I think you mean Reiki, right?" Lori replied.

"Yes, that's it," Mrs. Murphy said. "Can you do it? Jackie told me to close my eyes while she was doing it, so I'm not sure what she did. Can you figure out how to do it? Maybe Jackie can show you. I'd really like to keep getting it. It made me feel good all over."

1. Introduction

Alternative therapies continue to grow in popularity. Physicians like Bernie Siegel, Andrew Weil, Deepak Chopra, and Larry Dossey have become celebrities with best-selling books on alternative therapies. In 1997, 42% of Americans surveyed stated that they had used alternative therapies.[1] Approximately three-quarters of the British public believe their National Health Service should provide alternative therapies.[2] The proportion of Dutch people visiting alternative therapists more than doubled between 1981 and 1990, increasing from 6.4% to 15.7%.[3] Other European countries report between one-third and one-half of their populations using alternative therapies.[4] In Australia, 48.5% used alternative therapies in 1993, and this increased to 52.1% in 2000.[5]

This interest has spawned a multi-billion dollar industry. David Eisenberg and co-workers' frequently cited article reported that in 1990 Americans spent $9.4 - $13.2 billion on alternative therapies.[6] Their 1997 survey found expenditures had increased to $17.2 - $24.6 billion. Additionally, $5.1 billion was spent on herbal medicine, and $4.7 billion on therapy-specific books, classes, and equipment, bringing the total out-of-pocket expenses to $27.0 - $34.4 billion.[7] The American dietary supplements market was estimated at $17 billion in 2001, although the market hit a plateau in 1999 after years of growing annually by 20%.[8]

Many health insurance companies now provide coverage for alternative therapies.[9] Financial pressures often contribute to providers offering alternative therapies. Rising health care costs and cut-backs in services make

---

[1] Eisenberg, David M. et al. "Trends in Alternative Medicine Use in the United States," *Journal of the American Medical Association* 280.18 (November 1998): 1569-75.

[2] Fisher, Peter, and Ward, Adam. "Complementary Medicine in Europe," *British Medical Journal* 309 (July 1994): 107-10.

[3] Dijk, Paul van. *Geneeswijzen in Nederland.* Deventer: Ankh-Hermes, 1993; cited in Fisher 1994, 107.

[4] Furnham, Adrian. "Why Do People Choose and Use Complementary Therapies?" *Complementary Medicine: An objective appraisal.* Ed. Edzard Ernst. Oxford: Butterworth Heinemann, 1996, 71-88.

[5] MacLennan, Alastair H., Wilson, David H. and Taylor, Anne W. "The Escalating Cost and Prevalence of Alternative Medicine." *Preventive Medicine* 35.2 (August 2002): 166-73.

[6] Eisenberg, David M. et al. "Unconventional Medicine in the United States: Prevalence, costs, and patterns of use." *New England Journal of Medicine* 328 (January 1993): 246-52.

[7] Eisenberg, "Trends in Alternative Medicine."

[8] *Dietary Supplement Trends Report.* March 2002. Philadelphia: Natural Marketing Institute.

[9] Blecher, Michele Bitoun. "Gold in Goldenseal." *Hospitals & Health Networks* 71.20 (October 1997): 50-2.

alternative therapies look more attractive. Integration of alternative therapies into mainstream health care is seen as a way to boost diminishing income.[10] A 1994 study found that 69% of American chain drugstores and 3000 independent pharmacies stocked homeopathic preparations leading to $100 million in annual sales.[11]

Nurses also feel these pressures. Alternative therapies are portrayed as natural, gentler, and less invasive than medicine's drugs, surgery, and radiation. Hands-on, relaxation therapies are more compatible with nursing's traditional roots, in contrast to the cold, impersonal, computerized technology now dominating state-of-the-art health care. Alternative medicine's holistic philosophy is more in keeping with nursing's concern for the whole person, body, mind, and soul. Inclusion of spirituality within alternative therapies also attracts nurses. As one nurse stated, "Nursing must be open to nontraditional and alternative ways of healing."[12]

The direct patient contact which nurses cherish increases the chances of discussions concerning patients' health promotion practices. Nurses will likely be told about the alternative therapies patients use or are considering. Patients often have questions about these, making it imperative that nurses prepare themselves to respond ethically. As health care providers in whom patients place their trust, nurses have professional responsibilities regarding their responses to patients. This integrity becomes even more imperative when nurses become providers of alternative therapies.

This chapter's thesis is that alternative therapies create potential conflicts between two important professional responsibilities: being both patient advocates and providers of knowledge-based care. These two responsibilities do not necessarily conflict, but ethical dilemmas concerning alternative therapies often place them in conflict when defined in certain ways. This chapter will conclude that a Christian framework for patient advocacy provides significant practical guidance for responding to questions about and requests for alternative therapies. Rather than generating conflicts, this approach incorporates knowledge-based care into patient advocacy.

---

[10] Grandinetti, Deborah A. "'Integrated Medicine' Could Boost Your Income." *Medical Economics* 74.18 (September 1997): 73-99.

[11] McDermott, June H., Riedlinger, June E. and Chapman, Edward. "What Pharmacists Should Understand about Homeopathic Remedies." *American Journal of Health-System Pharmacy* 52 (November 1995): 2442-5.

[12] Sarvis, Connie. "Four Strong Winds." *Canadian Nurse* 90 (September 1994): 51.

129

2. Defining Alternative Therapies

Alternatives therapies have been defined as those with little clinical evidence supporting their efficacy or safety. However, this characteristic becomes less useful as more research is published on alternatives. Others distinguish alternative therapies by their underlying holistic philosophy, contrasting it with the "reductionistic" scientific approach of conventional therapies. This author has argued elsewhere that any ethical approach to health care must take all aspects of patients' lives into consideration, and science is needed to provide reliable information about all therapies, alternative or conventional.[13] Eisenberg gives yet another popular definition of alternative therapies "as medical interventions not taught widely at U.S. medical schools or generally available at U.S. hospitals." While always subject to change, this understanding includes the idea that alternative therapies are frequently "outside the pale" of established medical practice.

These definitions all suffer from including a wide range of practices. Eisenberg's list included, in decreasing popularity: relaxation techniques, herbal remedies, massage, chiropractic, spiritual healing, megavitamins, self-help groups, imagery, and commercial weight-loss programs.[14] A common-sense, conventional approach to healthy living would include many of these. Defining them as alternative therapies exaggerates the number of people using alternative medicine. This problem is demonstrated in the way most popular articles mention Eisenberg's results to justify the need for further research, use, or acceptance of alternative therapies. The promotion of alternative therapies in these ways raises ethical issues.

For example, a nursing article promoting acupuncture stated that "acupuncture treatment is becoming widely accepted as an alternative therapy. Indeed, 40% of Americans are reported to have sought some type of non-conventional therapy in the previous year."[15] The author cited a 1998 newspaper article. Using the results of general surveys to support a specific therapy's use is inappropriate. While Eisenberg's survey found that 42% of Americans used alternative therapies in 1997, acupuncture was the least frequently used of the sixteen therapies reported (at 1.0%).

Eisenberg's 1990 survey was similarly misused in the promotion of Therapeutic Touch (TT), probably the most popular alternative nursing therapy. Two reviewers claimed that 32% of those who saw an alternative therapist did so for energy healing. "This result indicates a greater acquaint-

---

[13] O'Mathúna, Dónal, and Larimore, Walt. *Alternative Medicine: The Christian handbook.* Grand Rapids: Zondervan, 2001.

[14] Eisenberg 1993.

[15] Cadwell, Vicki. "A Primer on Acupuncture." *Journal of Emergency Nursing* 24.6 (December 1998): 517.

ance with energy healing modalities such as TT than expected."[16] But Eisenberg's report stated that the "32%" referred to those who used energy healing (1.3% of respondents). Therefore, only 0.42% of respondents saw a provider for energy healing. Apart from the mathematical mistake, Eisenberg did not state what practices were included under "energy healing," making any application to TT inappropriate. His 1997 survey clarified that this category referred most frequently to the use of magnets for healing.[17]

Labeling practices like dieting, relaxation, spirituality, and self-help groups as alternative therapies suggests that conventional medicine does not value them, when it often does. Medical ethics, with its emphasis on physician-patient relationships, has developed within conventional medicine due to the recognized importance of holistic care. Lumping all these practices together results in dubious and questionable therapies gaining credibility and acceptance on the coattails of undeniably important factors like nutrition, exercise, and relaxation. For this reason, a less concise, but practically more useful, classification of alternative therapies will be used here.

3. Categorizing Alternative Therapies

Developed in detail elsewhere by this author, alternative therapies can be divided into five categories.[18]

- Complementary therapies are practices like nutrition, exercise, and spirituality, which contribute to people's health in the broadest conceptualization. They have not been part of conventional medicine because medicine accepted a more limited goal of treating primarily physically-based illness, not because it considered them unimportant.
- Scientifically unproven therapies have little scientific evidence to support their efficacy, but their proposed mechanisms of action fall within well-established scientific principles. These would include many herbal remedies.
- Scientifically questionable therapies also have little scientific evidence of efficacy, but their proposed mechanisms of action violate well-established scientific principles. These would include homeopathy and magnet healing.
- Life energy-based therapies are those said to work through the manipulation of a nonphysical, almost spiritual, "life energy." These include TT, Reiki, and many others.

---

[16] Mulloney, Steffanie S. and Wells-Federman, Carol. "Therapeutic Touch: A healing modality." *Journal of Cardiovascular Nursing* 10.3 (April 1996): 45.

[17] Eisenberg 1998, 1571.

[18] O'Mathúna and Larimore 2001, 135-41.

- Quackery and fraud deal with the deceptive or poorly informed approaches of certain promoters. They can occur with any therapy, but are particularly problematic with alternative therapies.

Clear-cut lines do not exist between these categories, and therapies will move between categories as they become better understood. Nevertheless, the categories assist in evaluating alternative therapies because each raises different questions. Placing a therapy in the most appropriate category will suggest the best approach needed to resolve the ethical issues surrounding its practice. To assist our analysis of nurses' professional responsibilities concerning alternative therapies, let us consider the case study described at the beginning of this chapter.

4. Patient Advocacy

When confronted with a case like Lori's, nurses must ask themselves serious questions to fulfill their professional responsibility to be advocates for their patients. The American Nurses Association (ANA) Code for Nurses views patient advocacy as one of the foremost roles of the professional nurse.[19] While nurses value advocacy, the concept itself has many definitions and is fraught with practical, ethical, and legal difficulties.[20] The United Kingdom Central Council for Nursing, Midwifery and Health Visiting (UKCC) Code of Professional Conduct states that practitioners should always act to "safeguard and promote the interests of individual patients and clients."[21] This view of advocacy is also central to Christian social justice. God's people are called to protect and nurture the vulnerable (Deuteronomy 10:17-19; 1 Timothy 5:3-8). Lori's professional responsibility is to promote Mrs. Murphy's best interests regarding Reiki.

The importance of *being* an advocate is not debated. The controversy relates to the purpose of advocacy and different perspectives on patients' best interests. What exactly are Mrs. Murphy's best interests? One approach, called "existential advocacy," is becoming popular in nursing literature. It states that "the patient is the one who decides what is in her or his 'best interest' in any situation."[22] Existential advocacy assumes that people's greatest good is self-actualization or self-empowerment.

[19] American Nurses Association. *Code of Ethics for Nurses With Interpretive Statements*. Washington: American Nurses Association, 2001. Available at http://nursingworld.org/ethics/code/ethicscode150.htm.

[20] Cahill, Jo. "Are You Prepared to be Their Advocate? Issues in patient advocacy." *Professional Nurse* 9 (March 1994): 371-5.

[21] *Code of Professional Conduct*. London: United Kingdom Central Council for Nursing, Midwifery and Health Visiting, 1992.

[22] Gaylord, Nan, and Grace, Pamela. "Nursing Advocacy: An ethic of practice." *Nursing Ethics* 2 (1995): 13.

Human advocacy does not just give the patient information and await his decision, it helps the patient to authentically exercise their [sic] freedom of self-determination. It helps them to become clear about what *they* want to do. Human advocacy insists that it is *the patient* who must ultimately decide what is in the patients [sic] best interests.[23]

The implications for nurses are clear. "The nurse is obliged to act in the patient's best interests on the basis that only the patient can define his or her best interests."[24] In this view, Lori should help Mrs. Murphy obtain Reiki because Mrs. Murphy believes it helped her, regardless of what Lori believes about Reiki.

Existential advocacy flows from the broader claim that people determine for themselves what it means to be healthy. Promoters of alternative therapies commonly assert that people can, and should, "create their own reality." One proponent claims that when people recognize this idea they attain a new level of consciousness. *"At this level of consciousness we can create anything we desire."*[25] In *Creating Health*, Deepak Chopra elaborates, "The mind makes reality. Outside our perceptions, thought, and experiences, reality has no validity…. We create our reality."[26]

Little surprise, then, that existential advocacy is used by some nurses to promote alternative therapies. "Most patients are open-minded enough to want to know more about or use complementary therapies. As their advocates and responsible health care providers, we must respond."[27] The response this nurse envisions is the incorporation of various alternative therapies into *standard* nursing practice. Two other nurses give this advice about choosing an alternative healer: "The patient should be encouraged to trust her or his own intuition and judgment about whether that individual healer is appropriate at that time. The encouragement to rely on her or his own ability to decide what is best is a type of personal growth and healing in itself."[28]

Existential advocacy is a postmodern notion. Postmodernism is a popular eclectic philosophy characterized by the denial of objective standards.[29]

---

23 Darbyshire, Philip. "Responsibility, Accountability and Advocacy: Student nurse dilemmas, Part II." *Irish Nursing Forum & Health Services* 7 (May/June 1989): 22.

24 Ellis, Peter A. "The Role of the Nurse as the Patient's Advocate." *Professional Nurse* 9 (December 1995): 206.

25 Brugh Joy, W. *Joy's Way: A map for the transformational journey: An introduction to the potentials for healing with body energies.* Tarcher, 1982, 20.

26 Deepak Chopra. *Creating Health.* rev. ed. Random House Audio, 1995, audiocasette.

27 Swackhamer, Annette H. "It's Time to Broaden Our Practice." *RN* 58 (January 1995): 51.

28 Engebretson, Joan, and Wardell, Diane. "A Contemporary View of Alternative Healing Modalities." *Nurse Practitioner* 18 (September 1993): 55.

29 O'Mathúna, Dónal P. "Postmodern Impact: Health care." *The Death of Truth: What's wrong with multiculturalism, the rejection of reason, and the new postmodern diversity.* Ed. Dennis McCallum. Minneapolis: Bethany House, 1996, 58-84.

Decisions are merely preferences based on arbitrarily chosen values—flavors in the smorgasbord of morals, not right or wrong. One's view of "health" is similarly up for grabs. "We must—as human advocates—assist patients to find meaning or purpose in their living or in their dying. This can mean whatever the patients want it to mean; ... Whatever patients define as their goal, it is their meaning and not ours, their values and not ours, and their living or dying and not ours."[30] Thus a patient's health "is defined by that patient and *dictates* the ensuing nursing actions"[31] (emphasis added).

Given this perspective, nurses who claim to have more expertise in an area, or a different opinion based on better evidence, should not press their concerns. "There are times when what is in the patient's best interests, as perceived by the health care professionals, is in conflict with the view of the patient, but that does not mean that the professionals should impose their own views. Patients' best medical interests are not necessarily their best interests as people.... Overruling patient wishes in such situations is blatantly paternalistic."[32]

Paternalism is viewed by many, especially within nursing, as clearly unethical. Yet ironically, existential advocacy is paternalistic. To allow patients to create their own meaning in health care, and make all their own decisions, is deciding for patients that their interests are best served by self-determination. But where is the evidence that this claim is so? Illness by nature sets up a situation in which power is unequally distributed. Advocacy assumes that someone with more power is looking out for the interests of those who are less powerful and vulnerable. Thus, it is so important that advocates exercise their power within ethical boundaries. Giving advice, even advising that the patient knows best, is a paternalistic act based on the advocate's values and training. The ethical issue is whether the advice given is truthful and reliable and actually in the patient's interest.

Claiming that health is defined by the individual, or "socially constructed," had wide-ranging implications, as noted here in a medical context: "If health and disease are nothing more than socially determined, culturally mediated and individually subjective concepts, then there will be little if any

---

[30] Curtin, Leah. "The Nurse as Advocate: A philosophical foundation for nursing." *Advances in Nursing Science* 1.1 (1979): 7.

[31] Gaylord 1995, 14.

[32] Ellis 1995, 207. Paternalism is the idea that patients should base their decisions on the advice of health care professionals ("doctor knows best"). This is justified by the professionals' greater knowledge or experience in health care matters. With increasing emphasis on patient rights and autonomy, paternalism is often viewed as unethical. While a full discussion of paternalism is beyond the scope of this essay, it will be briefly examined later.

possibility of either placing medicine on a firm scientific footing or of finding consensus among experts and patients as to the proper limits of medical concerns."[33] Taking a stand based on scientific evidence will be very difficult for nurses who hold to existential advocacy. [34] Deep internal conflict may result in trying to balance existential advocacy with the duty to care.[35]

Many alternative therapies are promoted through word-of-mouth, the internet, and other direct-to-consumer advertisements. Unfortunately, this information is usually incomplete and often designed to present only one side of the story. At times it can be distorted and even deceptive. Promoters and providers of alternative therapies have ethical and legal responsibilities to ensure that their advertisements are accurate. Similarly, the media must accept its ethical obligation to ensure accuracy in its stories about alternative therapies. Nurses should be willing to resist the pressure to recommend alternative therapies based on media releases or hearsay. In contrast to the postmodern notion that all standards are relative, therapy recommendations should be based on the most accurate and reliable evidence available.

5. A Christian Approach to Advocacy

The essence of postmodernism is the triumph of existential individuals creating their own values and beliefs based on any subjectively chosen criteria. One nurse commented on health care in the 1990s: "Perhaps one of the most exciting trends to emerge is that of the triumph of the individual."[36] Christian nurses should view this as problematic. It rejects the important Christian doctrine of humanity's fallenness and need for God. Throughout the Bible people's desire to decide for themselves what is in their best interests is viewed as the root of all human problems (Genesis 3:1-7; Judges 17:6; Romans 1:18-32).

Existential advocacy confidently declares that autonomy trumps every other ethical principle. In this view, "the right of self-determination ought not to be infringed upon even in the interest of health."[37] Advocacy based on Christian values cannot agree. Instead, the highest good is fulfilling the will of God. A patient's best interests are those that allow him or her to be-

---

[33] Caplan, Arthur L. "The Concepts of Health and Disease." *Medical Ethics.* Ed. Robert M. Veatch. Boston: Jones and Bartlett, 1989, 49-63.

[34] Some proponents of existential advocacy mention the need for accurate, objective data in promoting patients' best interests, yet do not wrestle with how this conflicts with their view that patients should determine their own best interests. E.g. Gaylord 1995, 15-18.

[35] Hylton Rushton, Cindy. "Creating an Ethical Practice Environment: A focus on advocacy." *Critical Care Nursing Clinics of North America* 7 (June 1995): 387-97.

[36] Sarvis 1994, 51.

[37] Gadow, Sally. "Existential Advocacy: Philosophical foundations of nursing." *Ethics in Nursing: An anthology.* Ed. Terry Pence and Janice Cantrell. New York: National League for Nursing, 1990, 43.

come all that God wants him or her to be. This belief requires that nurses be willing to speak the truth in love (Ephesians 4:15). The practical implementation of these ideas will vary between situations depending on the patient-nurse relationship. Biblical principles will directly apply to some situations and decisions, while others will benefit from little or no direct biblical counsel. Nurses should not start quoting Scripture to every patient. However, Christian nurses should be sufficiently knowledgeable of Scripture to be able to apply biblical principles without necessarily quoting Scripture.

6. Reiki

As Lori reflects on how to respond to Mrs. Murphy, she should be concerned about much more than just what Mrs. Murphy wants. She must start by investigating Reiki. She would learn that Reiki is a Japanese therapy said to have been practiced by the Buddha himself.[38] Knowledge of the practice was lost for centuries until a nineteenth century Buddhist monk "rediscovered" it during a psychic experience after meditating, fasting, and praying on a mountaintop for three weeks. Other details have been learned through channeling, a means of obtaining esoteric information by consulting spiritual beings called spirit guides.

Reiki comes from two words, *Rei* meaning spirit or source of life, and *Ki* meaning power or energy.[39] *Ki* (also called *prana* or *chi*) is a nonphysical, unconditional, divine, loving, healing energy.[40] When this energy flows properly in and through a person, health exists. If the flow is blocked, or unbalanced, disease arises. Reiki is done to restore the healthy flow of energy. During therapy, practitioners place their hands on or above the patient's body, keeping them in one place as they attune themselves to the life energy. Practitioners are viewed as channels, allowing the energy to flow through them and directing it towards the patient's energy field. Initially they focus on bringing about harmony and healing, but once the energy starts to flow through them, practitioners need not concentrate on what they are doing.[41] The energy flow gives patients sensations of hot, cold, tingling, color, or pain, and after a few minutes, practitioners "intuitively" know to move to another area. A complete healing session can take an hour or more.

[38] Stein, Diane. *Essential Reiki: A complete guide to an ancient healing art.* Freedom: Crossing, 1996.
[39] Wardell, Diane W. and Engebretson, Joan. "Biological Correlates of Reiki Touch[sm] Healing." *Journal of Advanced Nursing* 33.4 (February 2001): 439-45.
[40] Melwani, Lavina. "Rx: Reiki." *Hinduism Today* (January 1998): 38-9.
[41] Bullock, Marlene. "Reiki: A complementary therapy for life." *American Journal of Hospice & Palliative Care* 14.1 (January/February 1997): 31-3.

Reiki training involves a number of "initiation ceremonies" called "attunements."[42] These are "spiritual, sacred, and confidential rituals."[43] During attunements a Reiki Master calls upon spirit guides to open students' *chakras*, "energy centers" which transform the energy's frequency, eventually converting it into physical matter. Before Reiki training, most people's chakras are believed to be closed which prevents them from detecting this energy. The attunements open the chakras and fill trainees with life energy, often accompanied by sensations of heat in their hands. Trainees also intuitively receive special symbols which later become central to their healing practice, allowing them to increase the power of the energy. Until recently Reiki training was carried out in secret ceremonies, but is now promoted in popular books and nursing journals.

First degree Reiki practitioners can detect and move life energy in others. Second degree Reiki practitioners learn to use their symbols in treatments, and to send life energy over longer distances. They contact spirit guides and cooperate with them during healings. The third level, or Reiki Master, is traditionally attained after years of training with another Master during which practitioners commit their lives to Reiki, come to embody life energy, and give complete control of healing sessions to their spirit guides.[44] More recent efforts to introduce Reiki into mainstream health care differ here in claiming that all Reiki levels can be attained over a few weekends.[45]

7. Spiritual Truth in Advocacy

Reiki belongs to our fourth category, life energy therapies. Lori should be aware of the biblical injunction to test all spirits (1 John 4:1-3). Simply helping Mrs. Murphy express and realize her desires is refusing to view her as someone created in the image of God for whom he has a particular plan and purpose. Mrs. Murphy may still choose to pursue her own path and should be given the freedom to do so, but she should also be informed of the concerns and cautions Christians have about this category of therapies. Yet none of the Reiki articles in the nursing literature mentioned the role of spirit guides or the other overtly occult practices integral to Reiki.[46]

---

[42] Van Sell, Sharon L. "Reiki: An ancient touch therapy." *RN* 59.2 (February 1996): 57-9.

[43] Nield-Anderson, Leslie, and Ameling, Ann. "The Empowering Nature of Reiki as a Complementary Therapy." *Holistic Nurse Practitioner* 14.3 (April 2000): 21-9.

[44] Stein 1996.

[45] Nield-Anderson and Ameling 2000, 25-6.

[46] Bullock 1997; Van Sell 1996; Olson, Karin, and Hanson, John. "Using Reiki to Manage Pain: A preliminary report." *Cancer Prevention & Control* 1.2 (1997): 108-13; Sawyer, Jeannette. "The First Reiki Practitioner in our OR." *AORN Journal* 67.3 (March 1998): 674-7.

Everyone deserves to be informed of these aspects of Reiki as they may conflict with their religious beliefs. The Judeo-Christian tradition has always forbidden contacting spirit guides as part of its broader prohibition of involvement with the occult realm (e.g. Deuteronomy 18:9-14; Isaiah 8:19; Acts 19:18-19; 1 Corinthians 10:19-22). This prohibition remains in effect for Christians, but is also applicable to nonchristians. Biblical commands are not arbitrary rules issued by God to require some actions and prohibit others. God forbids certain activities because they are harmful for everyone. Involvement with spirit guides does not become harmful for those people who become Christians and choose to accept the truthfulness of biblical teaching. It is inherently harmful for all people, regardless of what they believe about it. For these reasons, this author believes Christians should neither practice nor receive Reiki. Yet some proponents of Reiki claim the practice has Christian roots.[47] Even a cursory examination of Reiki makes it difficult to support such claims.

A commitment to biblical truth should motivate Christians to share their concerns with others, regardless of whether or not they agree. We should have similar concerns for people harming themselves and others through alcohol abuse, illegal drugs, or other dangerous or unethical activities. However, this does not mean that Christians can compel others to agree with them. Just as people cannot be forced to become Christians, or alcoholics compelled to stop drinking, Christians cannot stop others' involvement in inappropriate spiritual practices. But they are called to voice their concerns and back them up with good evidence.

Once Lori is familiar enough with the teachings and practice of Reiki, she should be willing to explain her concerns to Mrs. Murphy, motivated by care and concern for her spiritual well-being. Lori's claim to know what is in Mrs. Murphy's best interests is, in some ways, paternalistic, although the gender-neutral term, "parentalistic," is more helpful here. This term emphasizes the power-differences involved in any patient-professional relationship. But it also reminds us that the "parental" person has an appropriate role in teaching and instructing. For the Christian, this need for input, instruction, and advice never ceases (Colossians 1:28). Neither does the call to approach others and disagree with certain decisions, motivated by love and concern for their well-being (Galatians 6:1). Lori's actions should not be an assertion of her opinions and wishes, but an expression of the truth of God's word applied to Mrs. Murphy's situation.

---

[47] Nield-Anderson and Ameling 2000, 21.

8. Scientific Truth in Advocacy

Lori's decision to consult biblical teaching was appropriate given the spiritual nature of the Reiki. But what about nonspiritual therapies, such as those in Categories 2 and 3? The Bible does not directly address these types of practices. Spiritual or not, alternative therapies claim to be effective, and the truthfulness of those claims can sometimes be tested. Lori should pursue this issue by examining the scientific research done on these therapies.

While science cannot prove anything absolutely true, it is a highly reliable method of obtaining accurate information about the physical world. Science attempts to describe and explain the regular patterns of behavior exhibited by the world's natural phenomena. Though its implications are sometimes said to be in conflict with Christianity, the scientific enterprise itself is completely compatible with Christian beliefs. The seventeenth century rise of science was influenced by many factors, prominent among which were Christian beliefs, including the intelligibility and goodness of creation, the importance of understanding nature through observation, and the value of scientific work as an expression of the "Protestant work ethic."[48]

A scientific approach to observation and reasoning forms an important backdrop to biblical claims about truth. God revealed himself in numerous instances by violating the regular patterns of natural activities. For example, Elijah's prayer to God resulted in his water-soaked sacrifice being consumed by fire, in contrast to the ineffective prayers of Baal's prophets (1 Kings 18). This demonstration is significant only if the onlookers had observed that wet matter does not spontaneously burst into flames. King Nebuchadnezzar demanded that his dream be interpreted without him revealing the dream to his magicians and diviners. They knew there was "not a man on earth who could declare the matter for the king" (Daniel 2:10). Daniel's accurate description of the dream revealed that his interpretation had a divine origin because "scientific" observations had demonstrated that human efforts to interpret dreams are completely unreliable. Most significantly, Jesus' healings were viewed as miracles because they violated the regular patterns and courses of diseases that people had long observed.

Hence, it is completely appropriate for Christians to rely on scientific information as a means of discovering people's best interests concerning therapies. Science is not a recent social construct of Western Enlightenment man, as postmodernists claim. Its basic characteristics have existed through-

---

[48] Barbour, Ian G. *Issues in Science and Religion.* Englewood Cliffs: Prentice-Hall, 1966, 44-50.

139

out history in people's attempts to understand and use their natural surroundings.

As with any human enterprise, science remains limited and fallible. In spite of all its discoveries, including numerous therapies which prevent, relieve, and cure illness, mistakes have been made. Science's limitations have, at times, been ignored or denied. In the form of naturalism or logical positivism, science has been viewed as the only source of reliable information. Under these ideologies science has been misused to devalue the nonmaterial dimensions of life, such as emotions, intuition, and spirituality. When those excesses were brought into medicine, nursing's attention to the nontangible aspects of health and healing were sometimes ignored, devalued, or even dismissed.

Some within nursing see postmodern ideology as a means to correct these excesses and restore a more holistic model to health care. Nursing is said to have an ally in alternative medicine since both have been "marginalized" by scientific medicine (represented by physicians). Western, scientific worldviews, or paradigms, are labeled as "male dominated, exclusive, authoritarian, linear, and rigid."[49] Science, it is alleged, is just a reflection of male, white, European prejudices. "Such paradigms require (indeed on a subconscious level they beg) to be overthrown."[50] Alternative therapies become very attractive in these power struggles as they usually do not require physician approval.[51]

But in reacting against the excesses of some scientists, postmodern nursing theorists swing to the other extreme and reject empirical science. "[E]mpiricism has been given the short shrift in nursing, because of continued fallacious identification with logical positivism, because of lack of familiarity with primary sources on the perspective, and because of the critiques rendered by hermeneuticists, phenomenologists, and critical social theorists."[52] These latter disciplines were foundational to postmodernism. Deficiencies in scientific understanding have long been acknowledged within nursing.[53] Instead of trying to correct these weaknesses, postmodern nursing devalues and rejects science:

---

[49] Daniels, Gareth J. and McCabe, Pauline. "Nursing Diagnosis and Natural Therapies: A symbiotic relationship." *Journal of Holistic Nursing* 12 (June 1994): 186.

[50] Daniels and McCabe 1994, 186.

[51] Thorpe, Barbara. "Touch: A modality missing from your practice?" *Advance for Nurse Practitioner* 2 (February 1994): 8-10; Schmidt, Carol M. "The Basics of Therapeutic Touch." *RN* 58 (June 1995): 50-4.

[52] Gortner, Susan R. "Nursing's Syntax Revisited: A critique of philosophies said to influence nursing theories." *International Journal of Nursing Studies* 30 (December 1993): 482.

[53] Jordan, Sue. "Nurse Practitioners, Learning from the USA Experience: A review of the literature." *Health and Social Care in the Community* 2 (May 1994): 177. Also, Naegle, Made-

140

[I]n recoiling from the male-dominated, reductionistic, disease-oriented biomedical model, nursing science has (perhaps unintentionally), narrowed its scope to study the social and behavioral sciences. In building a nursing science that devalues knowledge from the biological sciences we have "thrown the baby out with the bath water."[54]

The result is that in nursing "it appears that a tradition is developing where evidence is secondary to fashion."[55] If patient advocacy is to be based on anything other than fashion or opinion, it must be firmly rooted in reliable evidence about the effectiveness and safety of therapies. In spite of the postmodern claim that intuition, mysticism, and the paranormal describe the natural world as well as science,[56] the vast majority of effective therapies have been developed through scientific methodology. While Westerners are enamored by ancient Ayurvedic remedies with no scientific basis, native Indian Ayurvedic practitioners prescribe pharmaceutical drugs seventy-five percent of the time.[57]

The UKCC professional practice guidelines states, "The registered practitioner ... must be convinced of the relevance and accountability of the [complimentary] therapy being used and *must be able to justify using it in a particular circumstance*, especially when using the therapy as part of professional practice"[58] (emphasis added). In spite of their limitations, scientific studies remain the best method of justifying a therapy's use.

9. Ethical Issues in Gathering Scientific Information

Scientific studies sometimes demonstrate that alternative therapies don't work or are no better than placebos. Some within nursing claim these critiques are based only on "ignorance and a lack of dissemination of information."[59] They call for a level playing field by claiming that conventional therapies have little scientific evidence to back up their claims. In promoting alternative therapies, one nurse notes that "proponents of complementary

---

line A. "Prescription Drugs and Nursing Education: Knowledge gaps and impli-cations for role performance." *Journal of Law, Medicine & Ethics* 22 (Fall 1994): 257-61.

[54] Drew, Barbara J. "Devaluation of Biological Knowledge." *Image: Journal of nursing scholarship* 20 (Spring 1988): 25.

[55] Luker, Karen A. and Kenrick, Maria. "An Exploratory Study of the Sources of Influence on the Clinical Decisions of Community Nurses." *Journal of Advanced Nursing* 17 (1992): 463.

[56] Phillips, John R. "Inquiry Into The Paranormal." *Nursing Science Quarterly* 9.3 (Fall 1996): 89-91.

[57] Cassileth, Barrie R. *The Alternative Medicine Handbook: The complete reference guide to alternative and complementary therapies*. New York: W. W. Norton, 1998, 26.

[58] UKCC. *Guidelines for Professional Practice*. London: United Kingdom Central Council for Nursing, Midwifery and Health Visiting, 1996, 33.

[59] Daniels and McCabe 1994, 189.

therapies point out that only 15% of today's accepted medical interventions are supported by such solid scientific evidence."[60] This claim raises an issue in the ethics of professional writing: authors must ensure that literature cited actually supports their claims.

The 15% statement is based on a 1978 report made to the US Congress.[61] The claim itself, however, was not the conclusion of a scientific study, but a remark made by a member of a committee evaluating clinical decision-making in Britain.[62] The basis of the remark was a 1963 British survey of 19 physicians conducted immediately after British regulations for medication efficacy were introduced. This claim has since become an "urban legend" among promoters of alternative medicine. In contrast, more recent studies have found that the majority of medical decisions *can* be supported by solid scientific evidence.[63] Regardless of how well clinicians adhere to research-based evidence when making decisions, the proper response to deficiencies should be a call for more research and better adherence to the evidence, not the acceptance of more therapies with little or no supporting evidence.

The situation with Therapeutic Touch (TT) is a good example here. In spite of much contrary evidence, TT is promoted as effective and safe. TT practitioners claim to manipulate human energy fields (as with Reiki) bringing about relaxation, pain relief, and healing. Proponents claim it is the best researched of the nursing alternative therapies.[64] Yet external reviews of this research have consistently found little empirical support.[65] A prominent TT researcher, who remains convinced of TT's clinical value, summarized the current status of TT's research base:

---

[60] Swackhamer 1995, 50.

[61] Office of Technology Assessment. *Assessing the Efficacy and Safety of Medical Technologies.* Washington: Office of Technology Assessment, 1978.

[62] White, Kerr L. "Letters to the Editor." *Lancet* 346 (September 1995): 837-8.

[63] Michaud, Gaëtane, et al. "Are Therapeutic Decisions Supported by Evidence from Health Care Research?" *Archives of Internal Medicine* 158.15 (August 1998): 1665-8; Nordin-Johansson, A. and Asplund, K. "Randomized Controlled Trials and Consensus as a Basis for Interventions in Internal Medicine." *Journal of Internal Medicine* 247.1 (January 2000): 94-104.

[64] Thorpe 1994, 8-10.

[65] Walike, Barbara C. et al. "attempts to embellish a totally unscientific process with the aura of science …" in Letters, *American Journal of Nursing* 75 (August 1975): 1275, 1278, 1282; Clark, Philip E. and Clark, Mary Jo. "Therapeutic Touch: Is there a scientific basis for the practice?" *Nursing Research* 33 (1984): 37-4; Claman, H.N. *Report of the Chancellor's Committee on Therapeutic Touch.* Denver: University of Colorado Health Sciences Center, 1994; Meehan, Therese C. "Therapeutic Touch as a Nursing Intervention." *Journal of Advanced Nursing* 28 (July 1998): 117-125.

What current research about TT tells us ... is that there is no convincing evidence that TT promotes relaxation and decreases anxiety beyond a placebo response, that the effects of TT on pain are unclear and replication studies are needed before any conclusions can be drawn. Other claims about outcomes are, in fact, speculation.[66]

Proponents admit that they have no scientific evidence that the energy field even exists.[67] The American nursing organization devoted to promoting TT opposes certification of practitioners because (among other reasons) "energy flow can not currently be measured objectively."[68] An experiment in which TT practitioners attempted to detect people's energy without being able to see them found that practitioners detected the energy field no more reliably than would be expected by chance.[69] In spite of this, the influential textbook, *Nursing Diagnosis*, rejected criticism of TT and recommended its acceptance as a way to "celebrate the diversity among us."[70] If this is the basis for acceptance and advocacy of therapeutic agents, a wide variety of useless and harmful practices will be introduced.

In making recommendations about therapies, a thorough knowledge of the most recent literature is essential.[71] Nurses must often rely on secondary journal articles to gain this knowledge. This reliance places an ethical duty on authors of articles to ensure their information is accurate and current. Articles about controversial alternative therapies should present both sides of the debate so that nurses can evaluate whether or not to incorporate the therapy into their practice. Frequently, this balance is not exhibited.

Nursing journals use anecdotal stories to add a more personal dimension, but these also end up promoting unproven therapies. For example, a nurse recounted why she left nursing to become a craniosacral therapist.[72] She listed many conditions that she now treats, including headaches, sinusitis, head injuries, and accident trauma. Yet no mention was made of the controversial nature of this therapy which claims to regulate cerebrospinal

---

[66] Meehan, Therese C. "Quackery and Pseudo-Science." *American Journal of Nursing* 95.7 (July 1995): 17.

[67] Krieger, Dolores. *The Therapeutic Touch: How to use your hands to help or to heal.* Englewood Cliffs: Prentice-Hall, 1979, 57; Janet F. Quinn, R.N., Ph.D., cited in Jaroff, Leon. "A No-Touch Therapy." *Time* (21 November 1994): 88-9.

[68] Nurse Healers-Professional Associates. *Position Statement of TT Certification/Credentialing.* Philadelphia, nd.

[69] Rosa, Linda, et al. "A Close Look at Therapeutic Touch." *Journal of the American Medical Association* 279.13 (April 1998): 1005-10.

[70] Carpenito, Lynda Juall. *Nursing Diagnosis: Application to clinical practice.* 6th ed. Philadelphia: Lippincott, 1995, 356.

[71] For an excellent example of advancing patients' interests and avoiding harm by scientifically evaluating an alternative practice, see Youngkin, Ellis Quinn, and Israel, Debra S. "A Review and Critique of Common Herbal Alternative Therapies." *Nurse Practitioner* 21 (October 1996): 39-60.

[72] Elsdale, Bethan. "On Duty." *Nursing Times* 92.28 (July 1996): 173.

143

fluid rhythms by moving cranial bones. Studies have found that different therapists come to different conclusions about the rhythms said to underlie the treatments.[73] A review of published research found evidence of its effectiveness scant and inconclusive.[74] Yet the nursing story advocates that all nurses "incorporate craniosacral therapy into their work."

A review of acupuncture for emergency room nurses stated that "the World Health Organization has listed more than 40 conditions that can be successfully treated with acupuncture."[75] The forty conditions were listed, along with references to some of alternative medicine's best-selling popularizers, but not scientific studies. Yet the author failed to cite the National Institutes of Health Consensus Statement on Acupuncture which concluded that "[a]ccording to contemporary research standards, there is a paucity of high-quality research assessing efficacy of acupuncture compared with placebo or sham acupuncture."[76] The Consensus Statement found sufficient evidence to recommend acupuncture treatment for only post-operative nausea, morning sickness, and dental pain. Evidence showed that acupuncture was ineffective for smoking cessation, yet the nursing article claimed referrals for this condition might be appropriate. Authors of articles in professional journals should rely on more academic, research-based sources of information, not the popular press, since their colleagues will use these articles making clinical decisions.

When review authors cite research articles, they should represent the findings accurately, and present evidence of any scholarly debate. This acknowledgment often does not occur when proponents of alternative therapies publish reviews. Numerous TT reviews were found which misrepresented relevant research in their attempts to promote TT.[77] Usually only studies supportive of TT's efficacy were cited, although many studies find it ineffective. Studies cited as supporting TT's efficacy sometimes actually found mixed or even negative results. Early studies with positive results were cited without mentioning that subsequent replications, sometimes by the same researchers, did not support TT's efficacy. Most disturbing of all, in a number of instances studies which found TT ineffective were cited in support of its efficacy.

---

[73] Rogers, J.S. et al. "Simultaneous Palpation of the Craniosacral Rate at the Head and Feet: Intrarater and interrater reliability and rate comparisons." *Physical Therapy* 78.11 (November 1998): 1175-85.

[74] Rogers, Joseph S. and Witt, Philip L. "The Controversy of Cranial Bone Motion." *Journal of Orthopaedic and Sports Physical Therapy* 26.2 (August 1997): 95-103.

[75] Cadwell 1998, 514-7.

[76] "NIH Consensus Conference: Acupuncture." *Journal of the American Medical Association* 280.17 (November 1998): 1518-24. Available at http://odp.od.nih.gov/consensus/.

[77] O'Mathúna, Dónal P. "Evidence-Based Practice and Reviews of Therapeutic Touch." *Journal of Nursing Scholarship* 32.3 (Third Quarter 2000): 279-85.

This type of misinformation makes it practically impossible for busy nurses to find accurate information concerning alternative therapies in secondary nursing literature. The Code of Ethics for Nurses notes that nurses have professional responsibilities to the public that require accurate information. An earlier version put it more bluntly, calling on nurses "to protect the public from misinformation and misrepresentation."[78] It appears that nurses need to be protected from their own literature. Yet these are the sources nurses should be able to trust to become scientifically informed patient advocates.

The UKCC guidelines state that nurses should only introduce alternative therapies that are effective *and* safe. TT review articles make statements like "therapeutic touch has no reported adverse effects,"[79] or claim TT is "safe and effective."[80] Informed consent statements for prospective research subjects claim TT has no adverse effects. Yet numerous other TT accounts, including those of the co-founder, Dolores Krieger, claim that adverse reactions to TT *do* occur. Krieger describes "energy overload" with symptoms of "increasing restlessness, irritability, and anxiety that may be expressed as hostility or felt as pain by the healee."[81] Other authors give numerous cautions which include avoiding use of TT on patients with fever or cancer, limiting treatments around the head and over burns, and doing short treatments with newborns, the elderly, and the frail.[82]

While alternative therapies are usually presented as natural and therefore safer, this is not necessarily the case. How a nontouch therapy like TT could cause physical harm and discomfort is difficult to imagine from a scientific perspective. But given the altered states of consciousness involved in TT and its close association with occult and mystical healing, these negative effects should be of little surprise to psychologists and Christians.

The growing evidence of adverse effects from many alternative therapies points to the need for thorough investigations into the safety of all therapies before making recommendations to patients.[83] Part of the ethics of patient

---

[78] American Nurses Association. *Code for Nurses With Interpretive Statements.* Kansas City: American Nurses Association, 1985.

[79] Benor, Rita. "Therapeutic Touch." *British Journal of Community Health Nursing* 1.4 (1996): 203-8.

[80] Mulloney and Wells-Federman 1996, 27-49.

[81] Krieger, Dolores. *Accepting Your Power to Heal: The personal practice of therapeutic touch.* Santa Fe: Bear & Company, 1993, 75, cf. 74.

[82] For a review, see O'Mathúna, Dónal P. "Therapeutic Touch: What could be the harm?" *Scientific Review of Alternative Medicine* 2.1 (1998): 56-62.

[83] Ernst, Edzard. "Direct Risks Associated with Complementary Therapies." Ernst 1996, 112-25.

advocacy involves realizing the powerful impact nurses' advice exerts over patients. To be their advocates, nurses must rely on the best available evidence, whether it is biblically based spiritual advice or research-based scientific advice.

10. Conclusion

Interest in alternative therapies appears likely to remain high, at least for the near future. Nurses will receive many questions about these therapies. Nurses also appear to be at the vanguard of health care practitioners providing alternative therapies. Nurses must be mindful of their professional responsibility to be knowledge-based patient advocates. A powerful movement exists to undermine traditional notions of advocacy, turning it into nothing other than empowering patients to satisfy their desires.

The Christian worldview affords an important ethical alternative by which nurses' professional expertise and patients' vulnerability are recognized. It calls on nurses to diligently and thoroughly investigate the spiritual and scientific claims of alternative therapies and report them accurately in their literature. Christian advocacy uses the best biblical and scientific information to serve patients and promote their best interests. In this way, nurses can fulfill their professional responsibilities concerning alternative therapies.

Discussion questions

1. Do you agree with the author's conclusion that Lori should not provide Reiki to Mrs. Murphy? Why or why not?

2. Do you think it would be appropriate for Lori to provide other complementary or alternative therapies (those from the other categories given in section 3 of this chapter)? How would *you* distinguish between appropriate and inappropriate therapies?

3. How would you describe the different types of advocacy practiced by Lori and Jackie? Which form of advocacy would most patients expect from you? Which do you think is more appropriate for a Christian nurse to exercise?

4. In what ways have you seen postmodern ideology applied in your practice? What sorts of effects have these applications had?

5. Does Lori's responsibility to act as an advocate for Mrs. Murphy differ in regards to spiritual therapies like Reiki versus pharmaceuticals? Explain.

10

Professional Responsibility Regarding Intimacy and Sexuality in Patient Care

Bart Cusveller and Dónal O'Mathúna

Vignette

Mrs. Cook, age 46, suffers from a spinal lesion caused by a traumatic car accident. She has been hospitalized for four weeks and is waiting to be transferred to a rehabilitation center. Mrs. Cook is almost completely dependent on nurses to help her with her daily activities, including the removal of bodily excretions. Nurse Ruth enters the room to help her change her underwear and the following dialogue takes place.

Ruth: Let me help you with your underwear.

Mrs. Cook: It's just awful that you have to help me with this. I hate other people moving my body around as if I were a little baby. It makes me feel so helpless. And it's embarrassing as well.

Ruth: Oh, come on, Mrs. Cook, I am only doing my job.

1. Introduction

1.1 Outline

Any nursing ethics textbook should address issues of sexuality and intimacy or privacy in professional patient care. Nurses sometimes have to touch the patient's body in places they would never touch other people in their usual social encounters. Part of nurses' professional responsibility, then, involves dealing with issues of privacy and sexuality. This chapter will clarify some of their responsibilities in this area.

Unfortunately, reports continue to surface that professional conduct is often less than adequate in this area. Problems range from insufficient sensitivity (as in our vignette) to criminal behavior such as sexual abuse. In between are situations where nurses are asked to help patients satisfy their sexual desires, as when disabled patients have asked nurses to help them find prostitutes. Nurses' professional responsibility, ultimately, is a moral responsibility. This chapter will identify the kinds of moral issues that confront nurses in this area and those that confront Christian nurses in particular.

The perspective from which we are discussing professional responsibility enables us to address issues concerning intimacy and sexuality in professional care, however difficult this subject may be. Clear Christian teaching addressing sexuality can be incorporated into nursing practice where applicable. This teaching enables us to understand the nursing of male and female bodies and it offers guidelines for professional conduct in dealing with such intimate situations. This chapter will propose guidelines that address intimacy and sexuality in nursing in a professional, ethically responsible way. The focus will be on what nurses are called to do and to be for their fellow human beings who are in need of care.

1.2 Sexual morality

What we perceive as moral dilemmas in nursing is strongly influenced by the mores of our society, particularly in regard to sexuality and intimacy or privacy. In today's society, sexual behavior is openly displayed in public. Many advertisements, TV shows, movies, fashions, public events, not to mention websites, leave little to the imagination. A society's view of sexual morality depends on ways of thinking about relationships and families, and about male and female roles. But on a deeper level it depends on ways of thinking about the relationship between and the importance of our bodily and spiritual existence. How society views these relationships impacts Christians, but biblical teaching on these issues should shape Christians.

We see only too often, even among Christians, that external appearances and physical health become the idols of some people's lives. As in other situations, good things can be pursued to excess. Part of this excess stems from a belief that you can do almost anything you want with your body because human dignity is grounded in the spiritual or "higher" aspect of personhood, to the exclusion of other aspects. Think only of the immense interest within our society in spirituality or the arts. Think of the idolization of personal autonomy or of our own individual experience. Not surprisingly, we find that these kinds of beliefs are reflected in the way people think about intimacy and sexuality.

One influential line of thinking suggests that virtually anything is permitted regarding the body: "If it is my body, then it is my body to do with as I wish." This line of thought gives supremacy to autonomy and often results in people focusing on their immediate experiences. The body becomes the primary means by which life is experienced, and that experience is evaluated by what makes one feel good. For example, how you decorate your body with piercings, tattoos, and even mutilations, or the way you use your body in sexual relations, or how you allow others to touch your body is really of secondary importance. What is of primary importance is that the person "in" your body is the only one who can decide what feels best. Therefore, you are the one to decide what to do with your body. If it "feels" good to you, go ahead and try it. If it doesn't feel comfortable, don't do it.

According to quite a different line of thought, our corporeality should be suppressed as much as possible. The underlying belief here is that the body is not what really counts in life. This perspective may even lead to a disdain for bodily existence, as expressed by someone's dress or the way someone rejects all sexual activity. These people may neglect to care for their bodies, or withdraw emotionally if nurses must touch them. In the view being considered here, embodied existence is downplayed and a person's spiritual existence exalted.

How then should we perceive the role of intimacy and sexuality in life? In particular, how should we perceive the role of intimacy and sexuality in nursing? In what way might a Christian ethic guide us in this matter?

Admittedly, the saying "there is nothing new under the sun" applies here. The first Christians in Corinth wrestled with a cultural situation comparable to our own. They asked the Apostle Paul questions about sexual matters both within and outside of marriage (1 Corinthians 5-7). Perhaps surprisingly, Paul did not primarily direct them to the seventh commandment ("Thou shalt not commit adultery"), but rather to human nature. His answer could be summarized as follows. A Christian sexual ethic is based on the two premises that man and woman belong together and that body and spirit belong together. When people love one another physically, spiritual love is involved as well, as is the love of Christ.

149

Thus, physical intercourse outside of marriage involves Christ in something he wishes to have no part in. Conversely, when people love each other spiritually, the body will often be involved. Physical contact between friends and family members is appropriate and healthy. When a man and a woman love each other, there is a natural tendency to bring the relationship to the next level, that of sexual intimacy. But as in all areas of relationships, there is a proper context in which this should be done. If taken outside that context, sexual relations will lead to pain and damage.

In this earthly existence, our spirit is embodied; it is embodied in one of two genders, male or female. The body of the believer is even called a temple of the Holy Spirit (1 Corinthians 6:19). When a person neglects the value of the bodily and, therefore, sexual, aspects of relationships, he cannot fully glorify the Spirit of God who dwells within him or her. The body and the spirit are both integral parts of the complete person. Therefore, according to the Bible, sexual intercourse integrating physical and spiritual love is not possible in any authentic sense with regularly alternating partners. According to Christian sexual ethics, spiritual love, physical love, and an enduring relationship between man and woman are inseparably connected.

A Christian perspective seeks a balance between the physical and spiritual dimensions of sexuality. On the one hand, the physical body is seen as part of God's creation, and therefore is good (1 Timothy 4:4). Christians can, and should seek to, honor God with our bodies (1 Corinthians 6:20). Christians should remember that our bodies are not ours to do with as we please (1 Corinthians 6:19). We are stewards of our bodies. The very value of our bodies, being temples of the Holy Spirit whom we have received from God, should motivate us to avoid unethical behavior, especially sexual immorality (1 Corinthians 6:18-19; Romans 6:13). Our bodies should be kept under control and directed, not become the sensory pilots of our lives (1 Corinthians 9:27).

1.3 Intimacy, sexuality, and privacy

The concepts of intimacy and, especially, sexuality are used in many different ways. Definitions are not easily agreed upon. However, to discuss the professional responsibility of nurses regarding intimacy and sexuality we must be clear about how we understand the concepts of sexuality, intimacy, and privacy.

Intimacy and sexuality are closely linked with both the spiritual and bodily aspects of people's existence. Concepts like intimacy, sexuality, and gender overlap and impact different aspects of human life, making them difficult to define. They are not attributes or qualities we can easily measure. To

150

complicate things further, they depend not only on the individual, but on that person's relationships with others. They grow and develop as people mature in their relationships.

But on the other hand, our existence as embodied, gendered, and sexual people does not begin when we reach a certain point in human relationships. Even if physical and spiritual closeness come gradually, they are never totally absent. And we always were and will remain male or female. Within the embodied and gendered character of human existence we identify and respect distinctions between and degrees within human relationships. Each level brings with it opportunities and responsibilities: opportunities to experience a certain dimension of human relationships, but also the responsibility to conduct oneself appropriately in that relationship. When a nurse decides to avoid getting too close to a patient, this choice does not make the possibility of that closeness go away. Its potential will always be an aspect of her relationship with the patient.

Before going further, we must still try to define the terms central to our discussion. Let us begin by noting that the term sexuality obviously does not just refer to having sex; its reference is broader than that. In our earlier section, we related sexuality to physical and spiritual love. On this line of thinking, it would be wrong to identify sexuality with genital intercourse. Sexuality is better defined more broadly as referring to all human interaction that reflects the fact that humans have been created as male or female. So, when one nurse has more authority over a patient than another nurse, just because of the nurse's gender, then sexuality has come to the fore. Some may speak of gender here rather than sexuality. Either way, a whole group of behaviors exists from general human conduct all the way to genital intercourse. These behaviors express cordiality, tenderness, and even erotic awareness, and may not lead to sexual intercourse, but are properly viewed as part of one's sexuality.[1]

Secondly, it should be noted that the term intimacy is rather broader than sexuality and does not automatically include sexual activity. Parents, for instance, can be very intimate with their children without any sense of sexual overtones. And, conversely, some kinds of sexual behaviors are devoid of intimacy. Furthermore, intimacy goes beyond the bodily aspects of human relationships. Certain aspects of one's family history or one's religious beliefs may be considered very intimate. Intimacy, then, is an important as-

---

[1] Ehrenfeld, M. et al. "Sexuality among Institutionalized Elderly Patients with Dementia." *Nursing Ethics* 6.2 (1999): 144-9.

151

pect of personal closeness or familiarity.[2] It can be expressed in physical touch, e.g. by holding the hand of a dying relative. It may be expressed in the awareness two bosom friends have of their gender when confiding their marital secrets to one another. And, of course, it can be expressed in the sexual intercourse of spouses. But, again, intimacy need not be physical; it can also be spiritual. The widow, who keeps her deceased husband's coat in the closet for years and years, is doing something that reflects intimacy. But there is no physical intimacy, let alone erotic intimacy here. Yet, it may be noted, that the physical reminiscences are never far away in the case of the coat–it used to cover his body–and even the sexual aspects of intimacy are not absent–it is her husband's coat.

There is a third point to make in relation to intimacy and sexuality. We propose to understand privacy as the possibility or opportunity to be intimate. Nursing care often seeks to find privacy for the patient when certain intimate interventions or conversations must take place. Most have felt the embarrassment of the patient in a six-bed ward who is greeted in the morning by the physician with a loud and cheerful: "And how is your bowel movement today?" Patients also require privacy in moments of intimacy with their relatives and friends. The difficulty of providing privacy should never allow nurses to neglect this aspect of care. In as much as privacy is conducive to patient's health and well-being–and it commonly is–nurses have a professional responsibility to secure it. Nursing codes of ethics usually espouse the importance of privacy. In most countries, moreover, this responsibility is legally and socially enshrined. After all, it is a good custom–and one that Christian nurses will embrace–to mutually respect personal and physical integrity.

1.4 Functional intimacy

The notion of privacy, as a precondition for intimacy and sexuality, leads us to consider the notion of shame. For nurses this concept is very important. The physical body–think of nakedness in this context–not only makes human contact possible (as it clearly does), but it also creates a *distance* between people. It provides a boundary between your immediate life sphere and mine. This distance may come in degrees, depending, for example, on the way in which people express their gender or their sexual nature. These degrees, furthermore, may be influenced by cultural factors. All the same,

---

[2] Mattiasson, A.C. and Hemberg, M. "Intimacy: Meeting needs and respecting privacy in the care of elderly people: What is a good moral attitude on the part of the nurse/carer?" *Nursing Ethics* 6.2 (1998): 527-34.

shame reflects the fact that a person's sphere of privacy does, indeed, belong to that person and not to anyone else. Hence, strangers asking intimate questions or touching someone inappropriately are "shameful" acts, violating that person's dignity. They are transgressions of the confines of one's area of personal intimacy.

The limits of someone's sphere of privacy, i.e., the distance between his personal area of privacy and someone else's, are not to be bridged by just anyone, anywhere, or at any time. There has to be a valid reason to cross those lines. In our private life, love is usually that reason. We welcome a cordial kiss or hug by a respected and trusted friend or family member. The distant aunt or uncle who just keeps hugging and kissing, however, is clearly invading our personal area of intimacy for insufficient reason. That behavior would be a violation of our privacy, maybe even on the verge of an intrusion. When this aunt's womanliness or this uncle's manliness plays a role in that unwanted or unwarranted intrusion, we could stray into the area of sexual harassment, which is inappropriate sexual intimacy.

These issues apply equally within the professional sphere. To justifiably enter a patient's sphere of privacy, i.e., bridge the gap of shame, a nurse needs a valid reason. "In most cases the [intimate or private] information must be disclosed if clients are to receive a proper service from the professional concerned," as ethicist Paul Wainwright puts it.[3] Nurses' professional aim of promoting the patient's health and well-being may provide such a reason. Without it any attempt to enter that sphere can produce disproportionate shame in the patient. It is also unprofessional and unethical. For example, a semi-paraplegic patient may need the attendance of a nurse while he is washing himself. However, the same act may be a violation of privacy in the case of a patient who is perfectly capable of bathing himself. In other words, intimacy between nurses and patients in professional nursing care is warranted only in as much as it serves the patient's well-being and health. Consequently, we could call it functional or professional intimacy.

Many (experienced) nurses may not see any problem here. But not so those unaccustomed to these practices, such as inexperienced nurses and patients(!). They may react to these settings with reluctance and shame. Nurses should realize that they may find such feelings in patients and perhaps even within themselves. Such feelings are part of who we are as embodied, sexual beings. They will never be completely absent and they will not go away just because we ignore or dismiss them. Nurse Ruth responded

---

[3] Wainwright, P. "The Observation of Intimate Aspects of Care: Privacy and dignity." *Ethical Issues in Nursing.* Ed. Hunt G. London: Routledge, 45.

unprofessionally when she told Mrs. Cook that she was just doing her job. Most patients would not feel understood or respected by such a response. Mrs. Cook was trying to communicate her feelings of defilement or her belief that her privacy has been invaded. Nurses gain access to patients' innermost selves, and with that comes the responsibility to respond with respect and care.[4]

In sum, nurses need to remember the distinction between the sphere of everyday human interactions and the sphere of personal privacy or intimacy. Patients' perceptions of actions that threaten their privacy or personal integrity may not be the same as those of nurses. At times nurses may think there are professional reasons for invading a patient's privacy, maybe by touching a patient's body or asking a personal question. But when the patient is not expecting anything of the sort, feelings of embarrassment, shame, or even worse may be induced. Those situations should be avoided for the good of the patient.

Sometimes it also works the other way around. By way of example, a male patient was hospitalized for three weeks of flat bed rest because of a spinal hernia. Each morning he laid in bed stark naked waiting for the nurses to come and wash him. After a few days, the nurses determined that the patient was quite capable of bathing himself. When the patient continued to request nursing help, the female nurses felt their sphere of privacy was being taken advantage of. They then assigned a male nurse to bath the patient. The patient quickly withheld his invitation to enter his sphere of privacy. This example shows that nurses and patients can experience differences between their ideas of shame and privacy. Moreover, sometimes these differences are not sharply delineated but blurred. Nurses must develop the professional skill of drawing appropriate boundaries and lines when interacting with patients. "Loss of dignity can be avoided if those involved maintain a serious and respectful manner towards the patients and carers involved."[5]

2. Professional responsibility regarding intimacy and sexuality

Nurses may encounter situations in patient care which require the determination of professional responsibility in regards to intimacy and sexuality. We will address some of these practical situations in the next section. First we need to address the question of nurses' professional responsibility. Many textbooks—and many nursing theories—claim that patients' sexuality is

---

[4] Mattiasson 1998.
[5] For a discussion in terms of dignity and respect, see Wainwright 1994, 50-51.

within the sphere that nurses must attend to professionally, but then they provide little more than physiological information and advice about practical nursing skills. Sarah Earle sees sexuality as integral to holistic care, but then asks "why nursing has ostensibly ignored the issue of patient sexuality."[6]

The nurse's professional responsibility begins with promoting the patient's well-being and health. This task consists of preventing, remedying, or easing the urgent effects of diseases, handicaps, or medical treatments as these impact the patient's capacity to perform basic activities of daily living. According to this description, then, it is not part of nurses' professional responsibility to prevent, remedy, or ease diseases or handicaps as such. That is the doctor's job. Nor are nurses responsible for the way in which the patient avails of his ability to perform basic activities of daily life. Of course, these matters are not as clear-cut in practice as they may seem to be in theory. But for the time being, this description will help us discuss dilemmas involving issues of intimacy or sexuality.

If our description of nurses' professional responsibility is more or less adequate, the nurse has a professional responsibility in regard to the patient's intimate and sexual functioning insofar as

- the patient suffers as a result of disease, handicap, or medical interventions directly affecting his intimate and sexual needs.
- intimate and sexual behavior is part of the basic activities of daily living.

Patients may have legitimate needs in the areas of intimacy and sexuality that nurses cannot legitimately meet in order to promote the patient's well-being. Intimate and sexual involvement with a patient hinders rather than promotes a healing nurse-patient relationship. As we discussed above, different relationships bring with them different opportunities and responsibilities. The nurse-patient relationship requires trust and some intimacy, but not to the same extent as a marriage relationship. Nurses must remain somewhat detached so that they can provide unpleasant care, move on to other patients, and return home to their intimate relationships within their families. Nurses who become intimately and sexually involved with their patients transgress the boundary that allows the nurse-patient relationship to focus on the patient's health and well-being.

One might ask whether a nurse-patient relationship might develop into an intimate, sexual one. This situation certainly can, and has, happened. But when the nurse is caring for a patient, the relationship involves a vulnerable

---

[6] Earle, S. "Disability, Facilitated Sex and the Role of the Nurse." *Journal of Advanced Nursing* 36.3 (2001): 434.

patient and a nurse in a position of power. All professions recognize the inappropriateness of developing these fiduciary relationships into intimate, sexual relationships. They begin on unequal grounds, which can create difficulties throughout the relationship. At the same time, we recognize that once the nurse-patient relationship has ended, the couple may decide to pursue an intimate relationship once some time has passed. In that case, if the couple decides to marry, the relationship may eventually even become sexual (given our underlying premise that Christianity teaches that sexual intercourse be reserved for heterosexual marriage–1 Corinthians 7).

In general, therefore, some patient needs should be redirected to the patient's private circle of family and friends. Other needs beyond the nurse's area of expertise should be redirected to the proper professional dealing with that kind of need. If a patient has a genuine fear of intimacy or a pathological sexual incapacity, the nurse might refer the patient to a psychiatrist or a medical specialist. As we discussed when concluding that nurses should not comply with requests for euthanasia, the nurse cannot simply say "no" and leave it at that (see Ch. VIII). She has a responsibility to provide optimal care and, hence, at the very least, to participate in the activities of observation and decision-making, even if it is not her responsibility to perform requested interventions. In general, nurses are unable to do the maximum for the patients. Often they have to settle for doing the optimum, that is, the maximum given the circumstances or the conditions of care.

Hence, the professional responsibility of nurses is limited. Clearly, there are diseases, handicaps, and medical interventions with direct consequences for the patient's ability to perform basic tasks of daily living, and in particular, abilities that impinge on his or her privacy or sexuality. These symptoms may apply to certain oncological, gynecological, urological, and neurological diseases, which affect the bodily parts, hormones, or nerve systems involved in sexual and intimate bodily functions. Nursing care can and should be given in such cases. A person who has had a hysterectomy will require nursing care for some time, including, presumably, support in coping with this intervention and its consequences for the patient's sexuality.

When diseases, handicaps, and medical interventions have consequences that impact the patient's bodily functions relating to sexual and intimate activities, these activities take on a different character, especially if the patient is hospitalized. Try to have some privacy in a six-bed room! The question here is where to draw the line in regard to the nurse's professional responsibility. The nurse must help the patient restore his bodily functions, but is she supposed to allow the patient to exercise those functions if they involve the performance of intimate and sexual activities?

Here we must ask whether sexual activities are, in fact, part of the basic activities of daily life. Are they activities that are needed for human health and wholeness? Some claim sexual expression is important for overall well-being and that sexual activities are not qualitatively different from other physical activities like washing or going to the bathroom.[7] In our view, sexual activities are not essential for human wholeness, or, at least, not obviously so. Sexuality, if understood in the narrow sense of having sex, unlike sleeping or eating, is not an activity that is required in order to satisfy a need that must be met. Certainly, in the context of marriage, those needs can be met in very satisfying ways. But some people are able to cope perfectly well without having those needs met.

If sexuality is taken in a broader sense, it involves much more than just fulfilling basic physiological needs, instincts, or passions. Sexual intercourse may be seen as a language for communicating love within a personal relationship (since body and spirit belong together). But the communication of love (be it through bodily contact or not) is of more fundamental importance to personal wholeness than the mere ability to perform sexual acts. Consequently, it is not part of the nurse's professional responsibility to support patients in their pursuit of sexual activities, unlike, for instance, the nurse's responsibility to facilitate the patient's breathing, eating, or sleeping. Such activities are required for human health and wholeness. In the case of sexual function, the nurse's responsibility is limited to observation, counseling, and decision-making and, if needed, to referral. Self-help groups and patients' associations may also provide valuable support in this area.

Furthermore, it may be noted that the broad sense of sexuality discussed above more or less overlaps with what we have referred to as the realm of intimacy. Nurses have no professional responsibility to help patients perform sexual activities (because they are not fundamental). They do have a responsibility to help patients cope with issues related to intimacy when affected by disease, handicap, or medical treatment. The reason is precisely because the need for intimacy is fundamental to human functioning and sexuality in the broad sense. Patients should be helped to cope with their impairments or hospitalization. Those who have undergone surgery involving their primary or secondary sexual organs will sooner or later need to discuss the consequences for their intimate relationships. Because a breast removal will usually affect a patient's intimate relationship with her spouse,

---

[7] Earle 2001, 433-40.

nurses have to anticipate the patient's need for support and counseling. To be sure, the physician has a professional responsibility to provide information to the patient, implying that nurses have to attune their interventions to those of the physician and help the patient cope with this information.

Nurses may have a professional responsibility regarding disease prevention and health education concerning sexual behavior. Many diseases, behaviors, and treatments can affect one's capacity for normal sexual activities. In community care, one might think of the prevention of venereal disease or AIDS. Then there is the example of mastectomy mentioned above. In mental health care one could think of sex education of mentally retarded and ill persons in order to prevent harassment and violence as well as unwanted pregnancies and the spread of venereal disease. Here, the dilemma arises as to the extent to which sex education encourages patients to engage in sexual activities. Suppose nurses were to educate teenagers about "safe sex." Would that teaching not influence their sexual behavior and possibly constitute undue interference? In that case, it might not be part of the nurse's responsibility. But if it is part of the nurse's responsibility to warn teenagers against the dangers of unsafe sex, is it not equally their responsibility to warn them against promiscuous and extra-marital intercourse? These are difficult questions. The way one answers them will depend on one's view of sexual morality and on the extent of nurses' professional responsibility.

3. Dilemmas

3.1 Introduction

Nurses may encounter moral dilemmas relating to intimacy and sexuality in situations involving relationships between nurses and colleagues or other health care workers, between nurses and patients, and between patients and patients.

As regards the first situation, relationships between colleagues, we may be brief. Although inappropriate intimate and sexual activities, including intimidation and harassment, do occur in health care settings, their proscription does not necessarily have to do with nurses' professional responsibility. That is to say, for a doctor to fondle or flirt with a nurse, or the other way around, is more a matter of social ethics or labor law.

Many collective labor agreements, much labor legislation, and many institutional policies contain rules to protect the employee's physical and personal integrity, especially against sexual infringements or aggression. Employees have the right and the responsibility to prevent and fight unwanted intimacy. Nurses are wise to immediately make clear that they will not tolerate such behavior and to report any transgressions to the appropriate supervisor or to the transgressor's superior. Health care institutions often have (and in many countries are required to have) a policy for dealing with transgressions of this kind, ranging from a serious warning to dismissal and even prosecution. Many institutions also have a special officer whose duties include dealing with such matters.

Intimate and sexual activities among nurses and other health care workers have no immediate repercussions in regard to their professional responsibilities. However, the same is not true in regard to such activities involving nurses and patients or patients and patients.

3.2 Nurses and patients

Sexual contact (subtle or crude) between nurse and patient is obviously problematic. Given our understanding of the nurse's professional responsibility, there can be no question that sexual contacts (such as help with masturbation) are unprofessional and unethical. Ethical codes of conduct as well as legislation and regulations in most countries explicitly forbid this kind of practice. Often professionals and institutions are required to take preventive measures to avoid these behaviors.

Clearly, these prohibitions are instituted in view of the unequal position of nurses and patients in relation to one another. Patients are dependent; nurses are in charge. This difference creates the potential for nurses to abuse their position. Intimidation, harassment, and violence are possible within nursing as, no doubt, within any social setting. However, in the particular case of nursing, sexual activity involving nurses and patients clearly damages the professional relationship–even if the activity is engaged in voluntarily. Evidence does not support claims that the patient would be better off if the sexual activity is engaged in for "therapeutic" purposes. Therefore, this kind of activity constitutes a violation of the nurse's professional responsibility.

Obviously, it is also possible for nurses to be harassed by patients, either at home or in an institution. Harassment is an umbrella term for all kinds of unwanted and erotically tainted forms of intimacy and sexual behavior. Examples are jokes with double and suggestive meanings, rude comments, as well as touching and molesting nurses, eyeing them, asking for kisses and embraces, and confronting them with pornographic magazines or videos.[8] It is important, first, for nurses to show where the line is

---

[8] Mattiasson 1998.

and to make clear that they want to have nothing to do with behavior that goes beyond that line. It is equally important, secondly, to discuss such issues with colleagues. They may have had similar experiences, and discussing them may help everyone to cope with them. Thirdly, it is important to report such behavior to team leaders/superiors/head-nurses. Institutions are often legally, if not morally, required to have a harassment policy, providing protocols and guidelines. Consequences for patients violating these guidelines range from a serious warning to termination of care. In addition, institutions normally have a person or committee with whom to lodge confidential complaints concerning matters of this kind.

Should nurses succumb to the temptation to indulge in sexual activities with patients, they are making a professional error. If a patient pressures nurses to get physically involved with him or her, they may object for reasons that go beyond appeals to conscientious objections. Legal regulations protect the patient from abuse and bad care, and similarly nurses are protected from abusive patients. Institutions, too, ought to provide health care workers with specific guidelines for professional conduct. In addition to the nurse's personal values and norms, such guidelines are of great importance in promoting professional responsibility. As important as codes, protocols, and procedures are, the time devoted to discussing these important issues in educational and clinical settings is just as valuable.

Discussions are not only necessary because these are emotional issues, but also because the issues involved are not always clear-cut. Indeed, the borderlines between justified (professional) intimacy and violations of nurses' professional sphere of privacy vary between people. Whether we feel that the patient is being intrusive or not may depend on one little thing or another. We all know stories of evident transgression, but in practice grey areas and borderline cases are more common.

One reason for differences are discrepancies between the nurse's understanding of the borderlines and that of the patient. The best rule of thumb is that person who is most protective of her or his privacy ought to be respected by the other. This applies whether or not each agrees on where the borderline lies. Simply put: when in doubt, don't! When the borderline is more difficult to draw, as when the patient expects to be hugged for comfort, we move within the "negotiation zone." In that situation the nurse and the patient have to explore and respect one another's expectations and opinions regarding the intimate aspects of patient care.

Elderly nursing home patients were asked to describe the conditions in which they perceived physical touch positively. Touch was perceived positively if it was (1) adequate to the situation; (2) no more intimate than patients desired; and (3) devoid of a condescending attitude.[9] If any of these factors were not met, patients perceived touch negatively. This study demonstrates the importance of privacy from the patient's perspective. To respect patients' privacy and dignity, nurses should explain what they plan to do and ask patients if they may proceed.

The situation may be especially difficult if the patient's dysfunction is linked to his or her sexual self or if self-control or decorum has been lost. This loss happens often in mental health care, whether it is within psychiatrics, geriatrics, or caring for mentally disabled patients. Suppose the patient is obsessed by one of the nurses. In such tricky situations, the nurse cannot easily withdraw from the nurse-patient relationship. The patient's dysfunction may be the very reason for their relationship. The patient's sexual behavior may be part of the reason why he was institutionalized in the first place. Nurses may have to continue to struggle with such situations while still maintaining a professional, caring relationship. However, these situations often involve practical or professional dilemmas rather than ethical ones (although such situations could not lead to ethical dilemmas, especially if nurses do not draw the line sharply and timely in response to intimate advances). Discussing these difficult situations with colleagues is vital if the nurse is to cope professionally. There may come a time, though, when a replacement nurse is needed, either on a short-term or permanent basis.

In our view, when the promotion of a patient's basic daily activities means involvement in sexual activities, we have moved beyond the realm of nurses' professional responsibility. If the patient is not in a position to have sexual contacts–because he is institutionalized, for instance–then the members of his own private circle should be asked to deal with this issue, just as they would for financial matters. We also believe it falls outside the realm of the nurse's professional responsibility to arrange opportunities for the patients to have sexual contacts with persons from their personal circle, even with spouses. While accommodation may be possible for spouses, many institutions do not have such facilities.

Some patients would like to have sex with other patients or even with prostitutes when hospitalized.[10] Nurses do not need to avail of conscientious objections in such cases. They have a professional reason for objecting to such demands. The arrangement of sexual contacts is simply not part of the nurse's professional responsibility. Such contacts do not have any rela-

---

[9] Mattiasson 1998.
[10] Earle 2001.

tion to the patient's health problem. (It may be added that prostitution is not only morally, but also, legally objectionable.) Hence, nurses are under no obligation to engage in activities with a view to enabling patients to have sexual intercourse. For nurses it is more important to understand the patient's needs and to monitor his or her health situation as well as possible. Observation, counseling, referral, search for alternatives, and reporting remain as important in this area as in others. Expectations may differ, warranting dialogue.

For nurses working in psychiatrics or caring for the mentally handicapped, intimacy may need to be handled differently. The need for intimacy and sexual activity may be an urgent matter for the patient since it cannot be met until he is discharged. Hence, general prohibitions of intimacy will not suffice. In particular, in caring for the mentally handicapped and children, nurses often are involved in more than the usual nursing care. Here, hugging could be a much-needed expression of sympathy and compassion for the patients, as well as demonstrating appreciation and encouragement.[11] Yet, the general prohibition against sexual activity between nurse and patient holds, even if the borderline between intimacy and sexual activity, on the one hand, and merely social intercourse, on the other, at times is not very clear. It is, therefore, of the utmost importance that the institution and the professional alike develop guidelines and protocols for dealing with the boundaries relating to intimacy and sexual activity in mental health care. It is incumbent on both to recognize the duty to curb temptations to engage in inappropriate intimate and sexual activities. Fortunately, in many countries, the need to regulate this aspect of care is becoming more and more recognized and subjected to disciplinary measures.

3.3 Among patients

Most things that occur between humans also occur between patients. Sexual and intimate behavior seldom has anything to do with why patients are hospitalized or how they are being cared for. Nurses, therefore, have no professional reason to interfere between patients choosing to develop mature relationships. However, patients are required to behave in ways compatible with the purpose of their stay in the institution. In practice, certainly during short stays, this guideline means abstaining from sexual practices. At the same time, it is the nurse's responsibility to protect the health and well-being of *all* patients. Nurses who believe a patient is preying on other pa-

---

[11] Ehrenfeld 1999.

tients must get involved to protect those patients. In general, then, the hospital situation does not, and need not, allow for sexual relations between patients.

The dilemmas relating to relations between patients tend to take on a special character in health care facilities involving long or permanent stays. Here it may become impossible to uphold the argument that sexual matters do not represent urgent needs. They do become such, even if not for everyone. In its broad sense, issues of sexuality will resolve themselves without becoming problematic. Sometimes, people in residential facilities, elderly as well as children, will find enough solace in the sense of security that a good friendship can bring.

Yet sometimes the patient's needs go beyond those of friendship and become clearly sexual (in the narrow sense). For moral reasons we reject sexual intercourse outside marriage, but in no way can we reject that intimacy and sexual activity may represent urgent needs for patients. We also rejected the idea that nurses have a professional responsibility to promote sexual contacts for patients. However, the question does arise regarding the extent to which nurses have a professional responsibility to provide opportunities for patients to have sexual contacts with others in a residential facility. Clearly, they have a general responsibility to protect the well-being of other patients. But if two residential patients have sex with one another, is that not a matter of privacy? Should the nurse not accept the fact that being admitted to a hospital inhibits the patient's personal activities? In other words, to what extent do nurses have a professional responsibility to provide residential patients with opportunities to have sex?

To answer this question let us begin by comparing the situation to that of other situations involving treatment and care. In general, a patient may feel that he or she has a certain need and asks for the means to satisfy it. However, the need may not be within the scope of nurses' responsibility. Patients may have many different needs, but not all their needs are necessarily needs to be met by the nursing profession. A dying patient who feels lonely may ask for euthanasia. That desire does not make the requested intervention a professional responsibility. It is the nurse's professional responsibility to consider the needs and the means to satisfy them in a professional light. It follows that it would be unwarranted to ignore or neglect a request for an undesirable means (perhaps by recourse to a conscientious objection) because that would mean ignoring a genuine need. The same goes for sexual needs. So, how is the nurse to proceed?

After having explored and understood the patient's needs as thoroughly as possible (after all it may turn out to be a genuine request or desire for sex), adequate means to address these needs should be sought and discussed with those involved. Remember that we are talking about long stay situations. This response may well involve some considerable educational skills. The means should also be in proportion to the problem. The remedy should not be worse than the disease, so to speak. A mentally handicapped person, who is sexually aroused by tensions in the group where he or she lives, should be helped by attempts to address the quality of the interactions within the group rather than by medication that suppresses arousal. Less burdensome means are better, which implies that nurses have to consider the alternatives. It would be wrong to use a certain means if there were better ones available. In some cases, medication might be the best option when all things are considered. To act in this way is very different from doing what the patient wants or just arbitrarily satisfying the patient's autonomy.

The difficulty is, of course, that in long stay patient care it can be difficult to distinguish between mutual friendship, therapeutic relationships, physical care, intimacy and security, as well as the sexual aspects of each. This ambiguity makes it hard to arrive at a once-and-for-all-solution on the basis of a fixed set of norms and values. Is physical intimacy and sexual activity always intrinsically linked to lasting male-female relationships in these situations? Certainly not in the case of mentally incompetent persons. So, either we might give in to a nondurable relationship or we might prevent sexual activities. Either way, we are looking at what constitutes a painful loss for the patient.[12] Here we face hard choices. When all the alternatives have been considered and tried, we may be forced to allow something we really do not want. We are not choosing between right and wrong, but between lesser evils, and we must decide something. We don't need to abandon our norms and values. Sometimes we are with our backs against the wall, without any clear-cut conclusion. What we have then is an example of living in our fallen existence that we cannot get around.

A most important principle in regard to patient relationships in residential facilities (as well as elsewhere) is that the well-being of other residents is part of the nurse's responsibility. Not every relationship will be right for, or harmless to, both parties or even to third parties. We stand on biblical teaching that sexual intercourse is inappropriate between anyone other than a married couple. God did not declare this principle to frustrate our sexual needs, but because sex outside of marriage is ultimately unhealthy for the whole person. But in a pluralist society, patients and colleagues may not

---

[12] Shelly, J.A. and Miller, A.B. *Called to Care: A Christian theology of nursing.* Downers Grove: InterVarsity, 1999. 74.

agree with our perspective. Written institutional policies and nursing care plans are important instruments in dialogues with patients and families involved. And insofar as the borderlines remain unclear, we repeat that they remain within the "negotiation zone." This is the zone between patient autonomy and nurse advocacy (cf. Chapter V).

If we sometimes have to help an incompetent patient in regard to certain intimate and even sexual activities within residential facilities, then by the same token it could be argued that we should assist the competent patient in long-term care in his quest for intimate and sexual activities. Perhaps this position is defensible, though we are not convinced it is. Some may see facilitation of sexual activities within the bounds of genuine social intercourse and a balance between rest and activity. This kind of assistance would not be directly linked to the illness or treatment of the patients. But it could be defended on the ground that hospitalization itself prevents the patient from living with his loved ones. Depending on the nature of the relationship under consideration, a facilitating role on the part of the nurse might perhaps be expected. If so, a separate room in the institution would be required, not only for the sake of the patient but also for the sake of other patients. After all, institutions provide rooms for other activities beside care and treatment, such as rooms to meet the family, watch television, or smoke. Nurses can make these other facilities available, especially for married couples. Whether these are made available for unmarried couples again raises the issue of living in a pluralist society where patients will chose what we as Christians view as inappropriate.

Christian nurses may argue along these same lines when facing other sexual or nonsexual behavior that is not medically unhealthy but rather is wrong or even sinful. That is to say, insofar as the needs fall outside the area of health and disease, nurses have no professional responsibility to attend to them. They belong to the personal sphere of the patient's life. It is only to be expected that nurses will meet patients with different norms and values, convictions, and lifestyles. We will usually not change these values and beliefs. However, the fact that a nurse does not approve of a patient's behavior does not mean that she does not have to care for him. A nurse should not walk away from patients, even if she finds it difficult to remain and care for them. The nurse's responsibility is to continue providing care and promoting healthier relationships. After all, patients may experience a conflict within their own value system and worldview that threatens their well-being. If so, the patient's need may fall within the scope of the nurse's professional responsibility.

As to the personal responsibilities of nurses, these fall outside the scope of the present chapter. It may be difficult to accept a patient's behavior if it falls outside your professional responsibility. When tensions rise to where nurses can no longer personally tolerate a patient, they must speak to their supervisors and perhaps appeal to conscientious objections. Thus, when objecting to certain kinds of sex education or to certain ways of discussing sex or helping with sexual matters, nurses may usually refer to relevant clauses of institutional policies or collective labor agreements.

Acknowledgement

The authors wish to express their gratitude to Kamalini Kumar of Clinton, Iowa, USA, for helpful comments on an earlier draft of this chapter.

Discussion questions

1. If Ruth were to apply the principles given in this chapter, how would she respond to Mrs. Cook's statement given in the vignette?

2. Is Mrs. Cook's concern related to sexuality, intimacy, or privacy, as the terms are used in this chapter? Would these distinctions provide practical help in an actual situation?

3. Do you agree with the premise of this chapter that nurses' professional responsibility does not include provisions for the patient's sexual needs? Why or why not?

4. Discuss situations in which you have seen patients' intimacy handled appropriately or inappropriately. What principles guide nurses to respond ethically?

5. How would the principles discussed in this chapter apply to a situation in which two male residents of a long-term residential facility requested a room to engage in homosexual activity? How would you respond to such a request in a public institution in a pluralistic society? Why?

11

Conclusion

Bart Cusveller, Agneta Sutton, & Dónal O'Mathúna

In our introduction, we indicated our aim: "to help Christian nurses toward a self-understanding that will promote confidence in their Christian values and assist them in articulating and defending those values in their often secular working environments." We proposed to do so by developing a Christian perspective on nurses' professional responsibility and applying it to clinical relationships and situations that may typically form the context of nurses' moral experiences. In such contexts we asked:

- What is nurses' professional responsibility here?
- What moral issues are nurses to expect here?
- What are nurses to do, think, and be in such contexts?

Our goal in this concluding chapter is to summarize the most important features of our account of the professional practice of Christian nurses. We seek to show how Christian nurses may put the findings of all these chapters into practice in a way that realizes both their professional knowledge and their Christian beliefs.

Our conception of the professional responsibility of the Christian nurse included three components: the qualities of the acting person (virtues); the acceptable, valuable, and desirable consequences of the actions (goods); and the principles or rules guiding the nurse's acts (norms). We will use this threefold distinction to highlight a few issues that the chapters in this book have addressed in the hope of helping the Christian nurse to exercise both commitment and responsibility.

First, we believe it is clear that a Christian perspective on the professional responsibility of the nurse is relevant since the aim of nursing is to promote the best interest of the patient. From this perspective the practice of caring is seen as part of rendering service to one's neighbor. The practice of caring is part of the nurse's serving vocation as a Christian. The Christian nurse sees herself or himself as a servant of both God and neighbors, a servant in the image of the Good Samaritan. The faith of Christian nurses informs their attitudes and serves as the basis for what we might call their virtues as clinical practitioners. Their faith guides them in the development of caring relationships with their patients. As the preceding chapters have shown, this faith, together with their professional knowledge and experience, also guides their responses to particular situations.

Thus, Chapter 3, for instance, brings to the fore the patient-centered attitude called for even in the most difficult and testing cases. This attitude is a central part of the nursing tradition, a tradition that is rooted in the Christian outlook of those who may be described as the "mothers of Western nursing," among whom we must include Florence Nightingale, a sincere believer. Chapter 4 illustrates how the nurse's Christian faith may encourage self-confidence and openness not least in encounters with non-Christian patients. Chapter 5 shows how the Christian faith helps nurses identify their professional duties as well as the limits of those duties. Other chapters show how the faith of the nurse yields guidance and direction; in addition faith fosters personal qualities, such as honesty, courage, and inspiration in morally complicated and distressful situations.

Secondly, our faith-based perspective shows how the Christian faith helps to foster good and professional patient care. Biblical values, goals, and promises beckon Christian nurses toward the patient's best interests when they deal with moral issues in the clinical context. The patient's best interest is the prime good or end nurses are trying to achieve. It determines their mode of action. In other words, the faith-based perspective adopted in this book highlights how Christian mores may inform the professional practice of the nurse and promote a truly patient-centered attitude. Not only does the Christian faith provide practical guidance, it provides a consistent rationale for the values and ends promoted. Biblical values and the Gospel message of God's love for humankind are not just abstract concepts or beliefs to be consigned to one's spiritual or religious dimension. Christian faith begins with accepting all that God offers to humanity, but God's love

168

should encourage and empower the Christian to respond in kind. Christian faith calls on humankind to respond in daily practice with love for God and with love and respect for one's neighbors. All these dimensions of Christian faith are beacons of light guiding Christian nurses in their dealings with colleagues and patients in the variety of clinical situations they face. In any situation that raises moral questions, confronts her conscience, or tests her patience, the Christian nurse must carefully assess how to respond both as a professional and a Christian.

This is illustrated in Chapter 6, where Christian nurses are encouraged to form good working relationships with their colleagues as well as with their patients. The chapter shows that if there are moral tensions between colleagues, respectful communication and cooperation and a willingness to listen to the other person are of the utmost importance. Similarly, Chapter 7 shows that a respectful attitude and a willingness to listen are important when working in multidisciplinary teams. The chapter emphasizes the importance of a working environment in which equality, fairness, and respect for others are prime values. It shows how the Christian nurse may play a role contributing to harmony and resolution of conflict situations by exemplifying precisely these values. Chapter 8 shows how the Christian nurse, by embodying Christian values, may promote good palliative care for those who are terminally ill. A respectful attitude, both towards patients and co-workers (even co-workers of different convictions), may set the scene for true palliative care, care promoting the best possible quality of life until its natural end.

Thirdly, a Christian understanding of the nurse's professional responsibility entails certain principles or rules. The main rule or principle is that embodied in the Gospel call for love and charity. Admittedly, the Gospel call for love of God and neighbor may not always tell the nurse exactly what to do in any specific situation. But living by this principle will develop the ability to appropriately put it into practice. Christian nurses who seek to act out their love for God and neighbor will know how best to be kind, caring, gentle, and patient towards their patients. The Gospel call for love will guide them in their approach to both patients and colleagues.

Of course sometimes the Christian nurse's own feelings about the right thing to do in a certain situation may come into conflict with nursing standards and generally accepted practices. Such conflicts may not always be easily resolved, since the nurse's belief or intuition regarding right and wrong may be hard to justify in words that will convince others. There are times, however, when Christian nurses must hold their ground by opposing certain practices accepted by colleagues and even contesting generally accepted standards. Indeed, if immoral practices that do not respect the life and well-being of the patient are enshrined in law or nursing codes, or are called for under the nurse's contract, Christian nurses have a moral responsibility to make it clear to colleagues that they will not cooperate in such practices. In most countries such conscientious objections to certain practices would be accepted. However, nurses or doctors who resort to conscientious objections often also seek to change the field of nursing or medicine in which they work to avoid having to face the kinds of situations in which they find it impossible to cooperate with their colleagues. Ultimately, however, the motivation to seek such changes should be patient-centered, fueled by a desire to provide better care for patients.

In addition to addressing palliative care, Chapter 8 examines the practice of euthanasia and considers whether nurses should cooperate with those who engage in this practice. According to a Christian outlook, every life is a gift from God. Thus every innocent person's life is to be cherished and protected. Our view is that Christian faith can lead to only one conclusion on this issue: a nurse or doctor should not act to deliberately cut short the life of a patient. The nurse and doctor working within a Christian or Hippocratic tradition should be respectful of all life, no matter how weakened or debilitated. This approach involves offering good palliative care that promotes the well-being of the whole person. Such care avoids both overly aggressive treatment that seeks to keep the patient alive at all costs, and it avoids the intentional termination of the patient's life. Difficult deliberations and agonizing decisions cannot be avoided, but in regard to euthanasia the Christian nurse's position is clear.

To highlight another issue, Chapter 9 offers guidance when deciding whether or not to engage in alternative therapies. In keeping with the principles of evidence-based practice, it is argued that unless such a therapy is scientifically sound, it should not be pursued. Nor should it be pursued if it is unsound from a Christian point of view. Although not typically a concern in a pluralistic setting, the Christian nurse holds that certain practices are spiritually harmful or dubious and therefore ought to be avoided. Chapter 10 deals with the question of how the nurse is to behave in morally ambiguous situations involving intimacy and sexuality. We argue that nurses neither have to nor should help patients have sex. Moreover, nurses should have very good reasons for invading a patient's personal sphere of privacy. Situations involving intimate encounters with patients call for great sensitivity. They require personal integrity on the part of the nurse as well as a gentle and detached approach. In this kind of situation nursing standards, as well as experience, will guide the nurse, as will her Christian outlook.

In other more mundane situations, the nurse may object to certain types of behavior on purely professional grounds, as when a colleague "borrows" supplies from the unit or even from a patient. Such behavior clearly violates professional standards. Even in this kind of situation, however, a Christian attitude will be of benefit. Aggression is seldom helpful, whereas a gentle approach may put colleagues at ease and lead to an honest discussion about the standards of nursing practice. This may then help colleagues see that certain things should not be done. This gentle confrontation may encourage them to act differently in the future, or stimulate their interest in how Christian faith helps people live by high moral standards.

Finally, to those who object to the writing of a book on nursing from a Christian perspective, let us just say that we have done so because we know that the Christian faith promotes the very attitudes that are called for in good nursing practice. In making this claim we do not seek to denigrate other faiths. We are not implying that nurses who come from other faith backgrounds or spiritual traditions may not be spiritually nourished by their faith in ways that are reflected in good professional practice. We are only seeking to show how the Gospel ethos may inform nursing and promote good patient care. Thus we do not apologize for writing from a Christian perspective but invite the reader to judge whether we have succeeded in showing how a Christian ethos may inform nursing practice for the better.

About the Authors

Contributors

Ann Bradshaw, R.N., Ph.D., is Senior Lecturer in Clinical Practice at Oxford Brookes University and Oxford Radcliffe Hospitals NHS Trust. She is author of *Lighting the Lamp* (London: Scutari, 1994), *The Nurse Apprentice, 1860-1977* (London: Ashgate, 2001), *The Project 2000 Nurse* (London, Whurr, 2001) as well as articles in various nursing, sociological, and medical journals.

Kees Kleingeld, Ph.D., is an ordained minister in a Christian Reformed Church in Wolvega, The Netherlands. He wrote a theological thesis in Dutch on the concept of responsibility in nursing (1996) and a subsequent textbook for nurses (*Beroepsverantwoordelijkheid in de verpleging*, Houten: Lemma, 1996), and contributed to the Prof.dr. G.A. Lindeboom Institute publication on nursing ethics (*Volwaardige verpleging*, Amsterdam: Buijten & Schipperheijn, 1999).

Arlene Miller, R.N., Ph.D., is Research Fellow, Nursing Department, Messiah College, Grantham, Pennsylvania, United States. Her publications include *Values in Conflict* and *Called to Care: A Christian theology of nursing* (Downers Grove: InterVarsity, 1990 and 1999, resp.), co-authored with Judith Allen Shelly.

Ada van Bruchem-Van de Scheur, R.N., M.N.Sc., is Research Associate and graduate student, Institute for Bioethics, Maastricht University, The Netherlands. She writes in Dutch on euthanasia and palliative care, also for the Prof.dr. G.A. Lindeboom Institute, and has published in the journal *Nursing Ethics*.

Fu-Jin Shih, R.N., D.N.Sc. (University of California, San Francisco), is Professor, College of Nursing, Taipei Medical University, and Director, Global Liaison Center, Taipei, Taiwan. Her publications include spiritual care, health needs, and organ transplantation research in *Journal of Advanced Nursing* and others.

Jan van der Wolf, M.Div., is Pastor, and Lecturer in Ethics, Christian University for Higher Professional Education in The Netherlands. He also contributed to *Volwaardige verpleging* (Amsterdam: Buijten & Schipperheijn, 1999) for the Prof.dr. G.A. Lindeboom Instituut.

Editors

Bart Cusveller, R.N., Ph.D., is Research Associate, Prof.dr. G.A. Lindeboom Institute, Centre for Medical Ethics, and Associate Professor of Ethics, Nursing Department, Christian University for Higher Professional Education, both of which are located in Ede, The Netherlands. He authored articles on Christian commitment and ethics in nursing in *Journal of Advanced Nursing, Ethics & Medicine, Christian Nurse International,* and other Dutch journals.

Agneta Sutton, Ph.D., is Associate Lecturer in Christian Ethics at University College, Chichester, and Visiting Tutor at Heythrop College, University of London, United Kingdom. She is married with four adult children. Her publications include *Man-made Man: Ethical and legal issues in genetics*, co-edited with Peter Doherty (Dublin: Four Court, 1997).

Dónal O'Mathúna, Ph.D., was Professor of Bioethics and of Chemistry, Mount Carmel College of Nursing, Columbus, Ohio, United States, during the time that much of his work on this volume was carried out. He is presently living in his native Ireland where he lectures on bioethics and alternative therapies at a number of universities. He is Visiting Professor of Bioethics at the University of Ulster, Coleraine, Northern Ireland. He has penned many articles on Christian ethics relevant to nursing and is co-author of *Alternative Medicine: The Christian handbook* (Zondervan: Grand Rapids, 2001).